Psychology for the Classroom: Behaviourism

Psychology for the Classroom: Behaviourism is a broad, unbiased and accessible introduction to behaviourist theory as applied to learning and education in a practical context. Focusing on contemporary issues and strategies, including the use of e-learning, the book provides a background to research in behaviourist theory and explains its implications for current teaching and learning, offering practical guidance to show teachers and students how they can use these ideas to improve classroom learning. Chapters incorporate:

- the history of behaviourist theory and key thinkers;
- pedagogical implications;
- practical strategies in the classroom;
- behaviourist theory and e-learning.

Case studies and scenarios demonstrating best practice are used to exemplify how theory relates to practice, showing how a carefully planned curriculum and reinforced behaviours lead to effective learning.

Appealing to practising teachers and education students alike, this book is a valuable and practical guide to the use of behaviourist theory in education, and is applicable to all those responsible for providing effective teaching and learning.

John Woollard is Lecturer in Information Technology Education in the School of Education at the University of Southampton. He has previously taught in both primary and secondary schools. He now researches teaching and learning with computers.

Psychology for the Classroom Series
Edited by Alan Pritchard and John Woollard
Consultant Editor: Matt Jarvis

The *Psychology for the Classroom* series is an invaluable aid for all trainee and practising teachers, and other professionals, who want to better understand the applications of psychology in educational practice. Providing an opportunity to explore key topics in educational psychology and apply them to everyday classroom practice, the series presents complex theory in an accessible and relevant way. Each book follows a set structure, introducing the topic, detailing and explaining the history of theoretical thought and explicitly linking theory to pedagogy and teaching. This series forms essential reading for all those responsible for teaching and learning who wish to make informed choices about their own pedagogical approaches.

Psychology for the Classroom: Constructivism and Social Learning
John Woollard

Forthcoming titles:

Psychology for the Classroom: E-learning
John Woollard

Psychology for the Classroom: Motivation
Ros McLellan and Richard Remedios

Psychology for the Classroom: Behaviourism

John Woollard

Routledge
Taylor & Francis Group

LONDON AND NEW YORK

First edition published 2010
by Routledge
2 Park Square, Milton Park, Abingdon, Oxon, OX14 4RN

Simultaneously published in the USA and Canada
by Routledge
270 Madison Avenue, New York, NY 10016

Routledge is an imprint of the Taylor & Francis Group, an informa business

© 2010 John Woollard

Typeset in Bembo by
Pindar NZ, Auckland, New Zealand
Printed and bound in Great Britain by
CPI Antony Rowe, Chippenham, Wiltshire

British Library Cataloguing in Publication Data
A catalogue record for this book is available from the British Library

Library of Congress Cataloging-in-Publication Data
Woollard, John.
Psychology for the classroom : behaviourism / John Woollard. — 1st ed.
    p. cm.
  1. Learning. 2. Behaviorism (Psychology) 3. Classroom management. I. Title.
  LB1060.W66 2010
  370.15'28—dc22   2009047621

ISBN10: 0-415-49398-6 (hbk)
ISBN10: 0-415-49399-4 (pbk)
ISBN10: 0-203-85142-0 (ebk)

ISBN13: 978-0-415-49398-7 (hbk)
ISBN13: 978-0-415-49399-4 (pbk)
ISBN13: 978-0-203-85142-5 (ebk)

Contents

Figures

Series preface

The focus of this series of books is the psychological elements of educational practice. The series aims to draw together and elucidate, at more than a superficial level, the major current topics of concern that are related to learning and to other important areas of psychological interest.

In the past teachers in training were introduced, at an entry level at least, to some of the psychology of learning and education. Although this element of the UK teacher training curriculum (TDA, 2007) has not quite disappeared completely, there is a considerably reduced emphasis placed on it in teacher training than was previously the case. Teachers currently in post report that they were not introduced satisfactorily to what they consider important aspects of learning – theory in particular – during their training (Pritchard, 2005). The relative success of *Ways of Learning* (Pritchard, 2005, 2009), and other books dealing with the same subject matter, can be seen as indicative of a need for more psychology for teachers and teachers in training.

In support of the wider rationale for the series, the work of Burton and Bartlett (2006) has some important points to make. They suggest that there is a danger that new ideas for pedagogical approaches in the classroom are often promoted, sometimes by government agencies, without the detailed research and theoretical underpinning relating to it being considered with due diligence:

> The speed with which the internet and television can transmit ideas and information and appear to afford them (often spurious) validation should concern us as educators . . . [they are concerned that] high-profile education consultants deliver courses on new pedagogies . . . [the presentations are] . . . drawn eclectically from a range of research findings thought to have practical benefits for learning [and that teachers] generally enjoy these stimulating sessions and the recipe approach to pedagogic techniques but

they are not encouraged to look deeper into the research that underpins them. (Burton and Bartlett, 2006: 44–45)

The books in this series aim to provide the opportunity, in an accessible and relevant way, to enable teachers, teachers in training and others with a professional interest in children, classrooms and learning to look more deeply at topics, background research and potential efficacy and to be able to make choices about their own pedagogical approaches and preferences from a position of knowledge and understanding. The authors will consider the needs of those in training to be teachers and are required to examine the theoretical and research basis for their teaching practice. This is important as it is increasingly the case that courses leading to Qualified Teacher Status (QTS) are linking assessed work to expectations of a master's level and awarding credits towards master's degrees. This is particularly the case with postgraduate-level teacher training courses.

The series, in turn, presents and examines the detail and potential of a range of psychology-related topics in the light of their value and usefulness for practising teachers. Each of the authors in this series presents an outline of the topic, a review of the research which underpins its principles, the implications of the underpinning theory for pedagogy and a consideration of strategies which teachers might employ if they wish to implement the precepts of theory in their teaching. The book's aim is to outline a trail from research and theory, to pedagogy and thence to teaching strategies in practice. There is a clear pedagogical element to the books. They present the ideas in the perspectives of research, theory, pedagogy and strategies for teaching. There are suggestions for further reading and activities, both of which are written to develop understanding and are classroom-based to develop skills and knowledge. The more general strategies provide teachers with sound starting points for developing their own particular plans for lessons and series of lessons including activities which will be informed by the principles of the topic in question.

Research is presented and explored; the theory generated by the research is outlined; and the pedagogical implications of the theory, leading to teaching strategies, follow. Within a set, but flexible, framework, individual authors have written in a way suited both to the requirements of teachers in training and the interests of teachers in practice.

Part of the intention of the series is to look beyond the charisma of the presenters of day courses, and similar, for teachers (Burton and Bartlett, 2006) and beyond the showy and commercialised publications aimed at selling expensive materials. Each book aims to give an evidence-based consideration of the possibilities afforded by new findings and ideas, a review of research upon which claims for teaching efficacy have been built and a solid foundation for teachers and those in training to build their own ideas and strategies. The new ideas and findings are presented in the context of existing knowledge, understanding and practice of the topic in question.

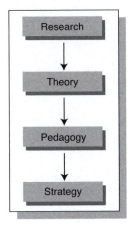

Figure 0.1 The conceptual path taken by each author when writing

Acknowledgements

I would like to thank my teaching mentors, colleague teachers, online friends and colleagues at the University of Southampton for their contributions and for 30 years of influencing and shaping my behaviourist views. In particular, I would like to thank pupils and students who, for those years, have been subjected to and have commented upon the behaviourist strategies of my teaching.

John Woollard
April 2010

1

Introduction

By the end of this chapter you will be able to:

- recall the important theorists of behaviourism;
- explain the terminology of behaviourism;
- describe the current views of behaviourism;
- use arguments to defend behaviourism against its critics;
- describe the underpinning principles of twenty-first-century behaviourism.

Behaviourism is a theory of animal and human learning that focuses upon the behaviour of the learner and the change in behaviour that occurs when learning takes place. Learning in the context of behaviourism can be defined as the acquisition of a new behaviour or the modification of behaviour as a result of teaching, training or tutoring. Learning is demonstrated by the behaviour of the learner in their actions or reactions to further stimulus.

Behaviourism has been a strong force in education from the early twentieth century through until the mid-1970s when the influence of constructivism and the social constructivist explanation of learning became vogue. Behaviourism remains an important focus of research, theory of learning, underpinning of pedagogy and the basis of classroom strategies. This book will place current practice and innovative ideas in the light of the behaviourist view of learning and show how the principles derived through the work of Ebbinghaus, Pavlov, Watson, Thorndike, Skinner and others remains an important influence in current teaching. This account of behaviourism is being made in the twenty-first century and can reflect upon the work taking place some 100 years previously. The importance and relevance of the work of those early educational psychologists can be seen in current and innovative practice in today's schools.

The language of behaviourism

Behaviourism is a philosophy, theory and pedagogy. They are underpinned by the principles of stimulus–response, and all behaviour is explained without the need to consider internal mental states or consciousness. However, those internal states such as belief, motivation and satisfaction can be represented by patterns of behaviour.

Conditioning and behaviour modification are both closely and most immediately associated with the behaviourist movement. Ivan Pavlov's classical conditioning is a form of associative learning where one behaviour or response is connected or associated with another to aid the learning process. It was first demonstrated by Pavlov, who repeatedly associated a neutral stimulus – the ringing of a bell – with a stimulus of significance – the presence of food – that caused his dogs to salivate. The presence of food and salivation by a dog are called unconditioned stimulus and unconditioned response. The ringing of the bell is a conditioned stimulus. Pavlov noticed that after conditioning the dogs would salivate on hearing the bell, even though there was no food present. This salivation is called a conditioned response. Although this form of classical conditioning has little direct application in the classroom, Pavlov's research and theorising identifies an important basis for behaviourist strategies.

Behaviour modification is a pedagogic approach whereby behaviour of a learner is changed by positively reinforcing (rewarding) an appropriate behaviour but ignoring inappropriate behaviour. Behavioural or operant conditioning occurs when a response to a stimulus is reinforced. The more the association between the stimulus and the response is rewarded, the more sustained the conditioning and the more likely that the response will occur in the absence of the reward. The removal of reinforcement altogether is called extinction. Extinction eliminates the incentive for unwanted behaviour by withholding the expected response. Some behaviour modification techniques also use negative consequences for inappropriate or bad behaviours. In those situations, behaviour modification works by conditioning children to expect positive reactions to or reinforcement of appropriate behaviour and to expect to be disciplined for inappropriate behaviour. However, many behaviourists believe that punishment is less of an influence upon behaviour than reward and that reward alone will be just as effective.

Behaviour modification assumes that observable and measurable behaviours can be changed. Behaviour analysis methods are developed for defining, observing and measuring those behaviours; the next step is designing effective interventions. Those interventions are based on the behavioural principles of conditioning through positive reinforcement that is rigorously applied and based upon consistent antecedents, contingencies or consequences. The process of operant conditioning is illustrated in Figure 1.1. The antecedent is pecking. Conditioning a behaviour occurs when the behaviour becomes associated with a reward. Interventions are designed to increase or decrease the target behaviour by making the association between wanted behaviour and reward stronger. Proactive behaviour modification is based upon interventions that avoid the use of aversive consequences and usually involves teaching new and more appropriate behaviours that are incompatible with the unwanted behaviour. For example, a child seeking attention by wrongdoing is discouraged by rewarding attention seeking associated with academic or social achievement. To reduce an inappropriate behaviour, an appropriate incompatible behaviour must be taught as the alternative.

Interventions include behaviour modification used to increase behaviour such as:

- rewarding (praise, celebration and approval);
- modelling, shaping;
- observation charts;
- token economy; and
- self-monitoring/sanctuary.

Interventions used to decrease behaviours include:

- extinction;
- reinforcing incompatible behaviour;
- self-monitoring; and
- shaping.

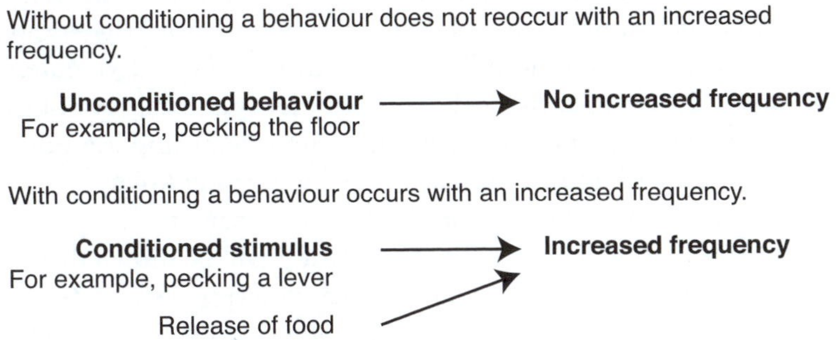

Without conditioning a behaviour does not reoccur with an increased frequency.

Unconditioned behaviour ⟶ **No increased frequency**
For example, pecking the floor

With conditioning a behaviour occurs with an increased frequency.

Conditioned stimulus ⟶ **Increased frequency**
For example, pecking a lever
Release of food

Figure 1.1 The process of operant conditioning

These are the tools of the behaviourist teacher.

Token economy, sanctuary and observation charts are methods employed to support and encourage the learner. They work in different ways, the first acting as a reward, usually extrinsic, for appropriate activity, the second as a more positive means of dealing with inappropriate behaviour and the third as a way to inform the learner and teacher about behaviour patterns, frequency and improvement. The behaviourist theory is based upon reward to change behaviour – that is the basis of the token economy in which appropriate behaviour is rewarded by a token to represent the reward. It is not always feasible or appropriate to be giving rewards of an immediate value. By giving tokens that represent rewards the same sorts of behaviour modification can be achieved as by the use of real rewards. The token economy can be highly sophisticated and institutionalised or very simple and informal. The rewards can be formally presented or, on the other hand, unceremoniously or covertly awarded. The rewards can be associated with a group or an individual; the system can apply to the whole school or be personalised and in place for just a single learner. The token economy is often associated with contracts or agreements between the teacher and learner whereby particular positive acts are rewarded by a token. Those positive acts can be the learner doing, being, appearing or completing in a predetermined way. The behaviourist theory suggests that punishing inappropriate responses is not as effective as rewarding the appropriate responses. The token economy facilitates the reward process.

At times, some learners find the constraints, distractions and obligations of the classroom too difficult. As a result they become off-task, poorly behaved, disruptive and even a danger to themselves or others. Adopting a sanctuary method to deal with such behaviour is a positive approach. The learner is given the opportunity to 'escape' in a pre-arranged agreement. The sanctuary could be sitting in a desk away from the other learners, sitting under the table, going to a 'chill-out' room or reporting to another member of staff. This is seen to be a more effective method of dealing with and resolving behaviour issues because the learner is identifying the symptoms, the triggers and the consequences of their behaviour. The learner may be allowed to strategically opt-out of social learning activities because they recognise that working alone can be more effective. These strategies have important implications when considering the social and emotional aspects of learning (SEAL).

Behaviourism as a learning theory has spawned many teaching strategies. Indeed, the influence has been so pervasive that it will be shown that a set of principles to underpin a comprehensive pedagogical approach can be devised. Task analysis, sequencing, modelling and shaping are four areas that illustrate the scope of that influence. Task analysis and sequencing relate to the process of curriculum development – how the learning activities are structured to maximise effectiveness. Modelling and shaping relate to the teaching process and strategies to enable learning by manipulating the learners' experiences. However, those four approaches are underpinned by the operant conditioning influences of positive reinforcement and the associated activities of measurement giving rise to the concepts of baseline, fading and maintenance.

Interventions are usually introduced after a baseline measure of behaviour has been established. Thereafter, the progress of an intervention follows typical phases. (See Figure 1.2.) After baselining, the intervention usually causes progress, and the appropriate behaviour increases. With most behaviours there is a natural limit that can be maintained. Most interventions are designed to be withdrawn and the behaviour level continues. Occasionally, when the rewards are withdrawn, the behaviour fades but the reintroduction of the intervention causes the behaviour to return to the maintenance level. The graph in Figure 1.2 does not have units on the axes because different interventions operate over different periods of time, and the measure of behaviour can be of different units. For example, an intervention to increase a learner's completion of homework or sitting through the story time would operate over 25 days and be measured each day. On the other hand, with the intervention designed to encourage collaboration, a judgement of collaborative behaviours would be judged every 15 minutes. The behaviour rate may be the percentage of the target level achieved or (inversely) the percentage of the unwanted behaviour that has been suppressed.

Modelling and shaping, in their simplest forms, are complementary.

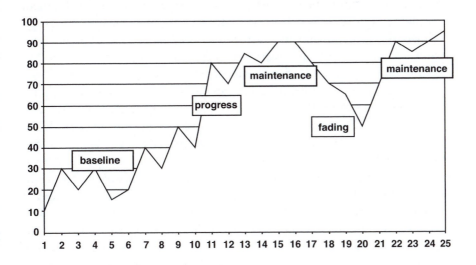

Figure 1.2 Phases of intervention

Modelling is showing the learner what to do, and they learn by copying or imitation. Shaping is making the learner carry out the behaviour, usually with repetition and through steps that enable the behaviour to gradually become the desired performance.

> Shaping is achieved through reinforcement of successive approximations of a desired behaviour.

A simple example is using the computer mouse. When a learner is first introduced to the mouse, they can learn through modelling. They see their parent, teacher or peer using the mouse to do things. They pick up the mouse and do similar things. If they are rewarded by success on the screen then they continue to do what they are doing, and learning continues through operant conditioning – appropriate behaviour is rewarded by success and achievement. If they are not successful they may watch other users to see what they are doing differently to improve their modelling, or the teacher may model appropriate actions for the learner to copy. The teacher may intercede and start to teach through shaping. In the case of using a mouse, the teacher may place his/her hand over the learner's hand and index finger and move the mouse and click the button through the child. The teacher shapes the patterns of behaviour. Stage by stage she introduces another aspect or refinement to the behaviour. An aspect of shaping is the combination of small elements of behaviour/knowledge in a particular pattern to create a whole of more significance. Shaping activities may result in the development of complex skills such as debate or understanding of concepts such as the solving of simultaneous equations. Maturation of skills such as social discourse occur through successive approximation as the first attempts are rewarded, but the same responses are not rewarded as they become less appropriate in the mature setting. For example, an adolescent saying 'I appreciate your support' would be rewarded but perhaps not for simply saying 'thank you'. Whereas a toddler would be rewarded for saying 'thank you' but not necessarily for saying 'ta'. An infant would be rewarded for saying 'ta' but not for saying 'da'. A baby would be rewarded for saying 'da' One of the many studies carried out by Albert Bandura was remarkable for showing the impact of modelling. In one of the Bobo the Clown doll studies, he filmed a young woman hitting and generally assaulting an inflatable, self-righting doll. As the woman punched the clown, she shouted a range of words, including 'sockeroo'. The film was shown to a group of 4 and 5 year olds before going out to play. In the play area there were some dolls and hammers. Within a short time many of the children were hitting the dolls with the hammers and shouting 'sockeroo'.

> Modelling is learning through imitation.

Because this learned behaviour did not fit easily with the traditional behaviourist viewpoint, Bandura developed an alternative theory of observational learning or modelling and eventually expounded the social learning theory. However, we can interpret the learners' activities as behaviours being reinforced by perceived or internal reinforcements. Behaviourists have no opinion upon or desire to understand that internal mentalistic process but accept that the processes of reward and punishment associated with intrinsic factors influence behaviour as strongly as extrinsic, tangible rewards and punishments.

Contracts and agreements are part of the pedagogy of behaviourism. They enhance and focus the processes of reinforcement and behaviour modification. A behaviour contract is an agreement between the learner and teacher about how the individual will behave. It indicates the consequence should the learner not behave according to the contract, and it also states the reinforcer that is used for successful compliance or completion. The behaviour contract provides the learner with structure and the opportunity for self-management leading to self-efficacy and is often an effective form of behaviour modification. Learning contracts include:

- the goal (learning outcome or appropriate behaviour);
- the methods or monitoring and recording;
- the method and conditions of reward;
- the consequences of not completing; and
- the time limits and process of review.

The sequencing of teaching activities is influenced by the behaviourist stimulus–response theories and a linear structure for instruction. This is often reflected in didactic approaches and forms of teaching that have little flexibility or personalisation. From the behaviourist perspective, learning is the complex development of stimulus–response that, like advanced shaping activities, make the whole more than the sum of the parts. To understand complex concepts requires the development of a linear chain of connections between the smallest units of learning. Task analysis is the process whereby those units of learning are identified. The teacher, through inspection and experience, breaks down complex topics into their component parts, identifies the stimulus–response activities and then chains these back together to form a teaching plan. This is called programmed learning and was the focus of, in the first instance, teaching machines (Skinner, 1968) and, more recently, computer programs for teaching spelling, numeracy and other rote-based activities. Task analysis is the strategic breaking down of a complex learning situation and the identification of the prerequisite learning necessary for the learner to succeed.

Post-millennium views of behaviourism

Behaviourism is the Cinderella of the learning theories. The second half of the twentieth century saw the growth of both cognitivism and constructivism as theories that can explain the phenomena associated with learning and also provide guidance for pedagogy. Although the truths and principles of behaviourism survive and, indeed, continue to develop, they are not overly represented in the academic literature and the writing of educational philosophers and psychologists. However, post-millennium views of behaviourism still exist, are widely articulated and are strongly held.

The University of Stanford continues to represent current thinking:

Analytical or logical behaviorism is a theory within philosophy about the meaning or semantics of mental terms or concepts. It says that the very idea of a mental state or condition is the idea of a behavioral disposition or family of behavioral tendencies. When we attribute a belief, for example, to someone, we are not saying that he or she is in a particular internal state or condition. Instead, we are characterizing the person in terms of what he or she might do in particular situations or environmental interactions (Graham, 2007).

'The Association for Behavior Analysis International (ABA International) is a non-profit professional membership organisation with the mission to contribute to the well-being of society by developing, enhancing, and supporting the growth and vitality of the science of behaviour analysis through research, education, and practice' (ABAI, 2009). On their website they describe the term 'behaviour analysis' as one that focuses on behaviour as a subject in its own right, rather than as an index or manifestation of something happening at some other level (in the mind, brain, psyche, etc.), after the work and endorsement of B. F. Skinner. He thought that the concept of mind belonged to the philosophers and that science should focus on behaviour, and these ideas form the core of behaviour analysis today (ABAI, 2009). The organisation is most widely represented in the United States but there are also international chapters and an annual international conference.

Sources for further reading: journals

The Analysis of Verbal Behavior

The annual issue of *The Analysis of Verbal Behavior* is for the 'original publication of experimental or theoretical papers relevant to a behavioral analysis of
verbal behavior' (TAVB, 2009). Topics include: elementary verbal operants,
multiple control, rule-governed behavior, epistemology, language acquisition,
pedagogy, verbal behavior research methodology, and others.

Behavior Analysis in Practice

The intention of this journal is to promote empirically validated best practices
in an accessible format. It contains 'empirical reports describing the application and evaluation of behavior-analytic procedures and programs; discussion
papers on professional and practice issues; technical articles on methods, data
analysis, or instrumentation in the practice of behavior analysis; tutorials on
terms, procedures, and theories relevant to best practices in behavior analysis;
and critical reviews of books and products that are aimed at practitioners or
consumers of behavior analysis' (ABAI, 2009). The journal is available online
at http://www.abainternational.org/BAinPractice.asp

Behavior Modification

Behavior Modification, formerly called *Behavior Modification Quarterly*, is a journal from Sage Publications (Sage, 2009) and reports on current scholarship on
applied behaviour modification. It has articles on assessment and modification techniques relevant to psychiatric, clinical, education and rehabilitation
settings. However, the focus of articles tends to be dealing with the special
educational needs of people with medical or psychiatric needs. Currently,
less is reported in the academic literature concerned with the application
of behaviourist techniques in mainstream education. The journal is available online at http://www.sagepub.com/journalsProdDesc.nav?prodId=
Journal200900

Journal of Behavioral Education

The *Journal of Behavioral Education* is a forum for the publication of research
on the application of behavioural principles and technology to education. It
publishes original empirical research and brief reports exploring behavioural
education in mainstream, special and adult education settings.

Journal of the Experimental Analysis of Behavior

The *Journal of the Experimental Analysis of Behavior* is an online journal primarily for the original publication of experiments relevant to the behaviour of individual organisms. It is published by Rochester University, New York, and is available online at http://seab.envmed.rochester.edu/jeab

The Behavior Analyst

The Behavior Analyst, ABA International's official publication, is published twice annually. 'In addition to articles on theoretical, experimental, and applied topics in behaviour analysis, this journal includes literature reviews, re-interpretations of published data, and articles on behaviorism as a philosophy' (TBA, 2009). The journal is available online at http://www.abainternational.org/journals.asp

Journal of Applied Behavior Analysis

The *Journal of Applied Behavior Analysis* is a psychology journal that publishes research about applications of the experimental analysis of behaviour to problems of social importance, including classroom teaching in mainstream and special schools. For example, a recent paper discusses the question: Do children prefer contingencies? It discusses the efficacy of and preference for contingent versus non-contingent social reinforcement during play (Luczynski and Hanley, 2009). The journal is published by Rochester University, New York, and is available online at http://seab.envmed.rochester.edu/jaba

European Journal of Behavior Analysis

The *European Journal of Behavior Analysis* is published by the Norwegian Association for Behavior Analysis, and is primarily for the original publication of experiment reports and theoretical/conceptual papers relevant to the analysis of the behaviour of individual organisms. The journal is available online at http://www.ejoba.org

School Psychology Review

School Psychology Review is a refereed journal with a primary purpose to provide a means for communicating scholarly advances in research, training and practice related to psychology and education, and specifically to school-based psychology. Many articles relate to innovative intervention and prevention strategies and the evaluation of these approaches. The journal is available online at http://www.nasponline.org/publications/spr/sprmain.aspx

Sources for further reading: books

William Baum, in his work *Understanding Behaviorism: Behavior, Culture, and Evolution* (2005), clearly describes the evolution of behaviourism from before Skinner's radical phase to the current philosophies that can encompass language, socialisation and culture. He brings a twenty-first-century perspective to that history and describes the values found in considering the ideas of operant behaviour, reinforcement, stimulus, shaping and chaining. Baum points out the radical behaviourists rejected the mentalistic terms of belief, expectation, hope and intention, saying they have no place in the science of behaviour. He continues by explaining that the realist's approach accepts the existence of such things as being worthy of scientific analysis by considering them as behaviours in the same way as any other physical, vocal or social behaviour. James Mazur, in his work *Learning and Behavior* (2006), examines learning in the classroom and in everyday life through the language and concepts of traditional and modern behaviourism. Although the book focuses upon the principles of behaviourism as supported by the experiments and reflections from the radical era, there are many references to twenty-first-century research including psychoneuroimmunology (the study of the interaction between psychological processes and the nervous and immune systems) (Ader, 2000), developing superstitious behaviours (Aeschleman, Rosen and Williams, 2003; Keinan, 2002), management (Ammerman and Hersen, 2001), the concept of commitment (Ariely and Wertenbroch, 2002), health issues (Bickel and Vuchinich, 2000; Bouton, 2000; Gottfried, O'Doherty and Dolan, 2002; Johnson and Brinker, 2001; Johnson and Bickel, 2003), support for stutterers (Bray and Kehle, 2001), the motivational impact of money (Bucklin and Dickinson, 2001; Jacobs and Hackenburg, 2000), computer skills training (Davis and Yi, 2004), shape/face recognition (Ekman, 2003) and developing physical skills (Zetou *et al.*, 2002).

There are many current publications outlining the use of behaviourism-based health and education strategies for supporting patients and learners. Garry Martin and Joseph Pear (2006) explore the theory and practical application of behaviour modification and its pedagogic techniques. Raymond Miltenberger's book (2008) is a comprehensive tutorial guide for teachers on the principles and procedures of behaviour modification. *The Behaviour Management Pocketbook* (Hook and Vass, 2004) describes strategies for classroom and behaviour management without making direct reference to the underpinnings and deals with the behaviour rather than the epistemological aspects of behaviourism. S. P. K. Jena's book, *Behaviour Therapy Techniques* (2008), provides a current analysis of techniques, research and applications of the principles of learning to change behaviour. Through the examination of the underpinning assumptions of behaviour therapy and the use of empirical evidence to illustrate points, Jena's book identifies the relevance of shaping, chaining, prompting, modelling and punishment in learning. Julie Vargas' book *Behavior Analysis for Effective Teaching* (2009) is a complete treaty of behaviourist approaches in the classroom and is highly recommended reading for a teacher planning the curriculum and teaching strategies for others. Vargas bases her writing on 30 years of classroom teaching and is now the president of the B. F. Skinner Foundation.

Current research and the philosophical analysis in the field of behaviourism is presented in works by Paul Cozby (2007), Jonathan Dancy (2000), Ralph Rosnow and Robert Rosenthal (2005), John Staddon (2001) and Rowland Stout (2006). Rowland Stout's work is a philosophical analysis of the concept of mind, thoroughly embedded within the domain of behaviourist thinkers such as Gilbert Ryle, David Hume, John Locke, B. F. Skinner, Edward Tolman and John Watson. In contrast, Dancy's work explores the area of motivation and the conflicting or contrasting issues of why we do things (the heart of the behaviourist doctrine) and why we should do things. It analyses the behaviourist outcomes of exposure to moral- and ethical-related stimulus. In this modern work there are echoes of Albert Bandura's analysis and interpretation of how people act and the impact of other people's actions on their behaviour. John Staddon, in his work *The New Behaviorism: Mind, Mechanism, and Society* (2001), recalls that behaviourism was the dominant movement in the first half of the twentieth century, culminating in the radical movement. He both explains and criticises that radical behaviourism, its philosophy and its applications to social issues. However, his new theoretical behaviourism attempts to move experimental psychology away from a focus on 'mental life' (Staddon, 2001: 93) towards the core of science, which he calls 'economical description of nature' (2001: 154). His work marks the current position in behaviourist development.

Although a relatively small voice in the education and psychology field, the behaviourists continue to have an influence in current thinking, and the behaviourist principles have much to guide pedagogy in our schools. The professional and practical advice arising from authors such as Janice Baldwin, John Baldwin, Deborah Du Nann Winter, Susan Koger, Bill Rogers, John Staddon and Julie Vargas stand as testimony to the continued value of behaviourist principles guiding and underpinning the pedagogy and practice of twenty-first-century classrooms and learning environments.

The people of behaviourism

Behaviourism, as a learning theory, can be traced back to Aristotle, whose essay 'Memory' focused on associations being made between events such as lightning and thunder. Since then there have been many key thinkers that have contributed and continue to contribute to the behaviourist thesis. Although their work has many facets and during their lives they have had (and some continue to have) an influence in different areas of teaching and learning, a key implication for classroom practice is associated with each theorist.

Hobbes (1588–1679)

Thomas Hobbes' work predates the traditional behaviourists who reject all forms of mentalistic considerations; he suggested that thinking is rule-based and is a process analogous to arithmetic. He claimed that no man can know by discourse alone (Laird, 1968: 145; Hobbes, 2008: 42–4) but the knowledge by which most men live is knowledge gained from experience, remembering past actions and what consequences followed them; in that sense he is a behaviourist. The implication is that we as teachers must take cognisance of prior experience when planning learning activities.

Hume (1711–76)

David Hume based his philosophy of learning on the idea that it is our knowledge, and not our ability to conceive, that is restricted to what can be experienced. Hume divides the objects of human reason into two domains: relations of ideas (beliefs) and matters of fact (Hume, 1748/1961: 322). To a traditional behaviourist, this would seem at odds with all learning arising from experience. Hume thought that we can form beliefs about that which extends beyond any possible experience, through imagination. The implication for the classroom is that, although behaviour can be modified and learning facilitated by preparing learners, there are beliefs that also influence the learner and the learner's readiness to be receptive to teaching.

Ebbinghaus (1850–1909)

Hermann Ebbinghaus was a German psychologist, and his research gave rise to the phrase 'learning curve' as a result of his seminal work on memory with the 'laws of frequency' and 'laws of recency' (which are described in Chapter 3). He brought a better understanding of the learning process by showing that higher mental processes can be studied and analysed using experimentation, establishing the principle that inner workings of the mind can be measured and explained by measuring and explaining the behaviour of the individuals. The 'laws of frequency' and 'laws of recency' have implications for medium-term planning and the structured revisiting of learning objectives and the value to mini-plenaries and plenary sessions in lessons.

Pavlov (1849–1936)

Ivan Pavlov was a physiologist and whilst studying the salivary glands of dogs noticed that they would salivate before the food reached their mouths. He called this a 'psychic secretion' and later coined the phrase 'conditional reflexes'. He went on to show how dogs could be taught to salivate on hearing a bell. He associated the bell with food by always ringing it when food was shown to the dog. This is classical conditioning. We as teachers should be aware that there are behaviours, habits or conventions of behaviour of learners that have been conditioned, and our actions may condition inappropriate as well as appropriate behaviours, such as the automatic lack of attention to the lesson the moment the bell rings.

Thorndike (1874–1949)

Edward Thorndike was an animal and human psychologist who identified that learning was a process of trial and error whereby in selecting a correct response and receiving reinforcements a connection is made. Through his experiments he established conditions of learning defined by three laws that indicate the effectiveness of learning (Thorndike, 1898). He identified that reward reinforced the behaviour and punishment reduced the behaviour. It was Thorndike who established that reward was more influential than punishment and established the value of exercising learned behaviour to ensure it is sustained. Making the learner ready for learning is important; once habits or appropriate behaviours have been established, they should be exercised to sustain them. Learning behaviours can be reinforced by success.

Watson (1878–1958)

John Watson was a psychologist who claimed that psychology was not concerned with the mind or with human consciousness but was solely concerned with behaviour, making the study of people the same as the study of other animals and so could be carried out objectively through controlled laboratory experiments. He helped define the study of behaviour in his 1913 article 'Psychology as the Behaviorist Views It' and emphasised the importance of learning and environmental influences in human development and human behaviour. He claimed that he could make an infant develop into anything he wanted by shaping the environment (Watson, 1913). Despite his highly focused view of psychology, he has influenced a significant branch of psychological study. An important implication is that having the right environment to nurture the learning enhances efficient and effective learning.

Hull (1884–1952)

Clark Hull was an experimental psychologist who devised sophisticated models of animal behaviour and some aspects of human psychology including aptitude testing, behaviour theory and hypnosis. He wrote of the principles of behaviour and brought meaning to the concepts of drive, drive reduction, incentives, inhibitors and habit strength. He considered satisfaction and need reduction to be important factors. He promoted a hypothetico-deductive experimental approach whereby both the hypothesis to be tested and the evidence/conditions that would prove the hypothesis are set out before the experiment. He also proposed theories relating to rote learning. Although Hull was a great contributor to psychology, his use of precise quantitative terms and formulae make it difficult to generalise from his work.

Tolman (1886–1959)

Edward Tolman was a behaviourist but made, at the height of the scientific, behaviourist approach to psychology, the case for considering those internal or mentalistic processes. Tolman recognised the value of considering purposeful, goal-directed behaviour and not limiting all consideration of behaviour resulting from cause and effect. Tolman demonstrated that his rats were capable of a variety of cognitive processes and reflected that language 'in general and introspection in particular are simply themselves behavior-acts which in the last analysis indicate to the observer the very same behavior-cues and behavior-objects which might be indicated by the mere gross forms of behavior for which they are substitutes' (Tolman, 1922: 52); he brought a consideration of language into behaviourism in his recognition of cognitive psychology. From his work stems the notion that the behaviourist approaches can influence the spoken word and the expressed attitude or opinion, as well as the physical act, and behaviourist approaches have their place and value in teaching and learning of personal, social and moral education.

Ryle (1900–76)

Gilbert Ryle was an analytical behaviourist with the view that actions such as thinking, remembering, feeling and willing are revealed through behaviour that can be categorised. He is critical of traditional behaviourist stimulus–response theory for being too rigid and overly mechanistic to provide an adequate understanding of the concept of mind. To him, the mind is the person's abilities, liabilities and inclinations, all of which can be seen in the way in which they behave. Again, similar to Tolman's work, there is an implication that behaviourist can teach in areas of attitude, motivation, choice and exploration as well as the more rigid pursuit of defined or prescribed behaviours. It is the measurement of attitude, motivation and other internal drives through the behaviour of the individual that establishes the bridge between the mentalistic and the behavioural.

Skinner (1904–90)

Burrhus Frederic (B. F.) Skinner was an American psychologist, advocate for social reform and poet. He is the figurehead of behaviourism with his philosophy based upon the idea that learning is related to change in overt behaviour, and those changes in behaviour (responses) are the result of an individual's response to events (stimuli) that occur in the environment. However, he extended Watson's stimulus–response theory to operant behaviour and placed a greater emphasis upon the impact of the environment upon behaviour and his radical behaviourism allows for private stimuli and private responses. The philosophy does not regard them as mental (mentalistic) just because they are private. The classroom implication is that behaviour can be modified and learning can be enabled through reward; that reward can be internal and arise from the satisfaction or satiation of a drive that is perceived by the learner but not seen by the observer.

Place (1924–2000)

Ullin Place was a philosopher-psychologist advocating a brand of analytical behaviourism restricted to intentional or representational states of mind, such as beliefs, hopes and intentions. Place called these types of mentality (Graham and Valentine, 2004) and proposed that higher-level mental events are composed out of lower-level physical events and will eventually be analytically reduced to these in the same way as radical behaviourists can represent higher order concepts and thinking in terms of physical behaviours. The implication is that verbal discourse is subject to operant conditioning and verbal response can be understood in similar terms as physical responses are analysed. The classroom-based reinforcement of the verbalisation of knowledge, understanding and attitudes can influence knowledge, understanding and attitude.

Quine (1908–2000)

Willard Quine used many ideas of radical behaviourism in his study of knowing and language. He supported the analytic philosophy tradition but, like the radical behaviourists, the analysis is based in empirical evidence. Quine bridged the gap between the cognitivists, by accepting some mentalistic ideas, and the radical behaviourists, by supporting the empirical methodology.

Bandura (1925–present)

Albert Bandura began his thinking about psychology in a behaviourist culture with an emphasis on experimental methods of observation, measurement and manipulation that avoided the subjective and internal processes. He found the assertion that all behaviour was caused by the environment a little simplistic and introduced the notion of reciprocal determinism that accepted the underlying behaviourist premise but added that human behaviour influences the environment, and importantly, human behaviour influences other people's behaviour. His work is influential in developing ideas of pedagogy associated with observational learning and modelling and in developing the social learning theory that proposes that people learn from one another, via observation, imitation and modelling. This acts as a bridge between behaviourist principles and cognition. It also enables behaviourists to encompass attention, memory and motivation but described in terms of outward behaviours. The work of Bandura brings implications for the way in which learners learn, and what they learn can be strongly modified and enabled by the examples of those around them.

Refuting the critics of behaviourism

There are many criticisms of behaviourism. Some stem from a misunderstanding of the principles, others because the critics perceive limitations of the theory and some because they are wedded to the more recent vogue of constructivism and cognitivism. The criticisms are cited but not referenced to protect the authors. It is a device whereby a defence of behaviourism can be established by responding to expressed criticisms.

'Behaviourism does not account for all kinds of learning, since it disregards the activities of the mind.'

Radical behaviourists do not disregard the activities of the mind! They simply state that scientific effort should be directed towards measuring and explaining the product of the mind – the behaviours exhibited. Skinner's statements that '[t]he interrelationships are much more complex than those between a stimulus and a response, and they are much more productive in both theoretical and experimental analyses' (1969: 8) indicates that there is more to behaviourism than the simple stimulus–response relationship:

The behavior generated by a given set of contingencies can be accounted for without appealing to hypothetical inner states or processes. If a conspicuous stimulus does not have an effect, it is not because the organism has not attended to it or because some central gatekeeper has screened it out, but because the stimulus plays no important role in the prevailing contingencies. (Skinner, 1969: 8)

The second citation illustrates radical behaviourism in that both theoretical and experimental analyses of behaviour explain reinforcement and the change in behaviour.

'It [behaviourism] views the mind as a black box in the sense that response to stimulus can be observed quantitatively, totally ignoring the possibility of thought processes occurring in the mind.'

Not true – analytical behaviourists simply do not need to pursue matters further than the extrinsic expressions of hope, guilt, interest and other mentalistic concepts:

> Behaviorism, with its emphasis on experimental methods, focuses on variables we can observe, measure, and manipulate, and avoids whatever is subjective, internal, and unavailable – i.e. mental. In the experimental method, the standard procedure is to manipulate one variable, and then measure its effects on another. All this boils down to a theory of personality that says that one's environment causes one's behavior. (Boeree, 2006: 4)

> 'One criticism of behaviourism is that the benefits of behaviour modification are only short term, instead of life long.'

It is true that behaviourists, through the focus on the outcomes of learning, are able to make accurate measurements and clearly identify such things as forgetting, habit strength, fading, rote learning, retention, etc., and because of the nature of scientific endeavour, short-term experiments are easier than long-term experiments and so are more frequently carried out. However, behaviourist approaches are also responsible for explaining complex and long-term behaviour changes, for example, complex skills such as turn-taking in verbal communication and long-term development of social skills by those with autism. In Chapter 2, current research into the effectiveness of behaviourist strategies for supporting children with autism is described. In Chapter 5, there is a vignette that describes supporting trainee teachers' high-level discussion skills.

> 'Behaviourism does not explain some learning such as that associated with language and the development of speech by very young children.'

From the behaviourist viewpoint, communication and language are complex behaviours but subject to the same rules as all other operant behaviours. Patterns of behaviour are established by modelling, sustained through reinforcement, suppressed and eliminated. Catherine Snow documented, in behaviourist terms, an explanation of the development of conversation between mothers and babies and the role of turn-taking (1977). In the research, Snow was able to show that the speech patterns of the mother were about the same at all ages, and none of the other features of the mother's speech style showed any abrupt change at the time the children started to talk. She noted that changes did occur much earlier, at about 7 months. The methodological approach, although based only on the analysis of behaviour, is able to reveal aspects of the complex relationships between mother and baby and the structure of communication between them.

'Learners are seen to be passive empty vessels waiting to be filled with knowledge'. 'The learner is depicted as a lone investigator'.

The same criticism of behaviourism is slated at all theorists prior to the current socio-educationalist vogue. What those critics fail to understand or, at least, reflect on, is that without the analysis and representations of Plato, Locke, the Gestalt theorists, Piaget and Von Glaserfield, they, the socio-educationalists, would not be in a position to move from the focus of our understanding of learning by the individual to considering learning in the context of many. They developed their ideas on the shoulders of the behaviourists *et al*. The new behaviourists are now re-proving their theories by standing on the shoulders of the social constructivists and expressing how learning is fostered through intrinsic and extrinsic reward, and thus, the reinforcement of learning-related behaviours of mind and body. Behaviourists accept that learning is a complex activity but they are determined in the idea that even complex behaviours can be analysed and explained in terms of the stimulus–response model and behaviour modification through reinforcement.

This reflection is one of many that have influenced the writing of this book on developing behaviourist-based pedagogy:

Behaviourism was centrally concerned to emphasize active learning-by-doing with immediate feedback on success, the careful analysis of learning outcomes and above all with the alignment of learning objectives, instructional strategies and methods used to assess learning outcomes. Many of the methods with the label constructivist … are indistinguishable from those derived from the associationist tradition. (Mayes and de Freitas, 2007)

The nature of behaviourism

Psychology is a science. Its methods range from controlled laboratory experiments with constants and variables and measured outcomes through to the qualitative analysis and rationalisation of the complex social setting of the human environment. Within such a discipline as psychology there is inevitably a difference of opinion as to the best or most effective approach but the eclectic stand is to say that each can contribute to our understanding of humans, human behaviour and the human condition. Through history, the nature, mores and fashions of psychology have changed with the blossoming of theory and methodology and the demise of one form in preference to another.

Behaviourism, being one of the earliest established theories that had a direct and profound impact upon education, has a special place in the history of psychology. Its heyday was in the first half and middle of the twentieth century but became overshadowed by the influence of the cognitivist and social constructivist explanations of learning that continue to dominate the methods of experimentation and the principles of pedagogy to this day.

There are two intentions of this book. First, it intends to redefine behaviourism in light of 50 years of cognitivist and constructivist influence upon our thinking. That redefinition will accommodate and acknowledge the values of cognitivism and constructivism but hold by the principles that the way in which behaviours are established, modified or suppressed is by changing the environment and that learning of whatever sort is recognised through changes in behaviour. It will also acknowledge and recognise the scientific advances in neuropsychology and accept that there are physiological explanations of behaviour.

The second intention of this book is to identify and celebrate the way in which behaviourist theory can continue to influence and direct pedagogy. It will show that the most effective and contemporary approaches to teaching can be effected by and enhanced by behaviourist thinking.

Behaviourism is ...

Behaviourism is supported by *empirical data* obtained through careful and controlled observation and measurement of *observable behaviour* under laboratory conditions or within defined *social environments* such as the classroom, workplace, community hall and home.

Behaviourism asserts that there are *direct parallels between animals and humans* in the way in which learning appears to occur, and that research can be carried out on animals as well as humans.

Behaviourism asserts that *from conception* the mind is influenced by the environment and experiences, and that the environment, experiences and actions of other people influence a person's *motivation and behaviour*.

Behaviourism asserts that all behaviour, no matter how complex, can be reduced to a simple *stimulus–response* association and new behaviour occurs through *classical or operant conditioning*; or the *modification* of old behaviour through *rewards* and punishments; or imitation of observed behaviour, called *modelling*. Rewards are more effective than punishments.

Behaviourism accepts that some rewards are *intrinsic* and are associated with internal senses of gratification (pleasure), well-being (absence of need) or moral correctness (righteousness) and that the outcomes of some internal processes (such as learning) evoke those rewards.

Behaviourism encompasses aspects of *affective domain* that are reflected in the physical domain (interest, curiosity, motivation, cooperation, attitude, belief) and that these behaviours are influenced by reward and punishment.

Summary

- The behaviourist movement has a long history and has influenced many areas of human life and endeavour.
- Behaviourism, in terms of learning, considers that it is through modifying behaviour and ensuring learners' preparedness for learning that the best outcomes will be achieved.
- Behaviourism embraces a pedagogy based upon precision, rigour, analysis, measurement and outcomes.
- Behaviourism is a pragmatic and practical philosophy rooted in observation and experiment.

Activities

- Consider, in the light of the content of this chapter, the major differences between the earlier and animal-related descriptions of learning with the modern behaviourism view of learning with reference to the behaviour aspects of understanding, emotion, motivation and socialisation.
- Consider the 'critics of behaviourism' section and your experience of people's attitude to behaviourism.

2 Research

By the end of this chapter you will be able to:

- identify the nature of the classic experiments that underpin radical behaviourism;
- appreciate the range of applications of behaviourism as represented by recent and past practice;
- identify the basis for planning teaching with regard to behaviourist theories.

In this chapter, we consider research in the area of the behaviourist classroom as well as revisiting the classic experiments and observations that underpin behaviourism. Some examples are drawn from the work of well-established psychologists within education from over the past century whereas others are drawn from more recent classroom practice. The seven different sources of empirical evidence illustrate different approaches to research in the area; they will then connect with the theories in the next chapter.

Research with animals

An underpinning principle of behaviourism is that human behaviour is similar to animal behaviour. The behaviourists' belief that how an animal reacts is exactly like how a human reacts is fundamental. It is accepted that the sophistication of human behaviours and the complexity of the combinations of the different rules makes our reflections upon our behaviour more detailed. Perhaps it is our unique position of being human that gives us the desire to see more into the stimulus and reactions made by humans than we can possible perceive of that of a dog where, with all the will in the world to understand, we are outsiders to their world of motivations. Both animal and human operate under the same rules but human behaviour is far more complex than that of a dog, and as a dog may perceive, its behaviour is far more complex than that of a worm. All animals and human beings have their place on the spectrum of behaviour sophistication but all are connected by underlying principles. Edward Thorndike's important work on animal intelligence was published in 1898 and marks for many the start of experimental psychology because it makes the strong connection between animal and human learning and the experimental analysis of learning.

Thorndike designed some simple experiments that demonstrated learning in animals that enabled the formulation of a set of principles that continue to guide pedagogy in our schools. He developed an objective experimental method that could systematically measure the mechanical problem-solving ability of cats and dogs. He devised a number of wooden crates (puzzle-boxes) that required various combinations of latches, levers, strings and treadles from which a hungry cat or dog would escape. After some trial-and-error behaviour, the cat learns to associate pressing the lever (stimulus) with opening the door (response). This stimulus–response connection is established because it results in a satisfying state of affairs – access to food (positive reinforcement).

Thorndike's initial aim was to show that the anecdotal achievements of cats and dogs could be replicated in controlled, standardised circumstances in the time of the burgeoning experimental psychology movement. However, he soon realised that he could use the apparatus to measure animal intelligence by setting repeating and different tasks and measuring the times it took novice and experienced animals to solve the problems. By setting the same task repeatedly for the same animal he could see the reduction in solving time that came with experience. Thorndike then compared these 'learning curves' in different situations and different species. Through these experiments he established a pattern of learning and described three laws relating to learning based upon the consequences of behaviour. The law of exercise states that learning is established because the stimulus–response pairing occurs many times. The law of effect states that the learning is sustained because it is rewarded. The law of readiness relates to the combining of activities to form a single sequence response thus leading to complex learning. These are discussed more fully in Chapter 3.

■ The law of exercise (practice) states that a response to a situation may be more strongly connected with the situation depending upon the number of times it has been connected (reinforced) and to the average strength and duration of the connection (reinforcement).

- The law of effect states that the association between a stimulus and a response will be strengthened or weakened depending upon whether a satisfier or an annoyer follows the response.
- The law of readiness states that a learner's satisfaction is determined by the extent of his preparation or preparedness, that is, his/her readiness for learning. This law has two aspects:
  — when someone is ready to perform an act, to do so is satisfying;
  — and when someone is ready to perform an act, not to do so is annoying.

Thorndike turned his attention to human learning with experiments that measured the efficacy of learning a skill and retaining knowledge. In a classic investigation he identified the influence of improvement in one mental function upon the efficiency of learning other functions. The method was to 'test the efficiency of some function or functions, then to give training in some other function or functions until a certain amount of improvement was reached, and then to test the first function or set of functions' (Thorndike and Woodworth, 1901). In the paper, Thorndike presents his own evidence and that of others to show that developing skills and knowledge in one area does not necessarily and automatically give enhanced skills and knowledge in seemingly connected areas. Only when the skills are most precisely the same do positive correlations occur between learning one thing and the impact upon another. Activities such as:

- accuracy in noticing misspelled words;
- accuracy in multiplication;
- acting quickly, such as noticing words containing r and e; or
- identifying semicircles on a page of different geometrical figures

do not have an interrelationship in terms of learning. Thorndike goes on to show that even more closely related activities such as the estimation of length of one object type of one length magnitude does not have a profound impact upon estimation of different objects of the same length or the same object with different lengths. It is through this precise behaviour analysis of learning that the elements of understanding, learning and skills can be identified.

Repetition and rote learning

One of the earliest psychologists to adopt the experimental approaches associated with the behaviourists, Hermann Ebbinghaus, pioneered the experimental study of memory and is known for the origination of the spacing effect, the forgetting curve, the learning curve and savings described in his 1885 book *Über das Gedächtnis* and its later translation, *Memory: A Contribution to Experimental Psychology*. The spacing effect refers to his observation that humans and animals more readily remember or learn items in a list when they are studied a few times over a long period of time, rather than studied more frequently in a shorter period time – spaced presentation versus massed presentation. The forgetting curve shows the decline of memory retention over time and relates to the durability of learning. The learning curve shows how quickly information is learned. The sharpest increase in learning occurs after the initial tries; this gradually levels out as the learner reaches the success criteria and further learning has little impact on retention. Savings refers to the amount of information retained in the subconscious even after this information had been completely forgotten and so cannot be consciously accessed.

Ebbinghaus was able to show that higher mental processes such as memory could be studied using experimentation and the observation of the impact of different stimulations and activities. He assumed that the process of committing something to memory involved the formation of new associations and that these associations would be strengthened through repetition. He developed a series of experiments whereby the participant tried to remember nonsense single-syllable words. He acknowledged that prior experience has a significant impact upon memory and learning and so wished to eliminate the possibility that the participant would remember the words because of their meaning. A nonsense syllable is a consonant-vowel-consonant combination, where the consonant does not repeat and the syllable does not have any prior meaning, for example, DAX, WUG or TUD. Some single-syllable words were not used, as they sounded similar to proper words or were a subset of a regularly used word.

Ebbinghaus was the subject of his own experiments because he did not want anyone to be subjected to the tedium of the activity. He tried to control all aspects of the learning environment, including doing the tests at regular times of the day. In the trials he randomly identified a number of syllables placed in a box. He would pull out each in turn and write them down in a notebook. Using a metronome and with the same voice inflection, he would reveal, read out and cover each item in turn. He tested himself by recalling the list of nonsense words. He made many repetitions of the experiment, changing the amount to be learned (number of words) and the amount of learning (number of repetitions). He also measured the accuracy of recall after a period of time (retention) and carried out further tests to see the impact of prior learning on the new learning. These simple but detailed experiments have stood the test of time and contribute much of what is known about rote learning and retention.

His research showed that:

- time required to memorise nonsense syllables increases sharply as the number of syllables increases;
- distributing learning trials over time is more effective than concentrating practice into a shorter period;
- items at the start and near the end of the list are more readily remembered (primacy and recency);
- even small amounts of prior learning makes relearning more effective;
- continuing to practice the activity after the learning criterion has been reached enhances retention.

In later trials he showed that replacing nonsense words with meaningful words increased the ease of learning and the rates of retention.

Learning from example

Behaviourism as a philosophy, theory of learning and pedagogic approach has grown a great deal since the radical phase beginning with the work of B. F. Skinner. One of the early developments came from the work of Albert Bandura, namely observational learning (modelling) and self-regulation. Of the many studies he carried out, one set stands out above the others – the Bobo the Clown doll studies (Bandura, Ross and Ross, 1961; Bandura, 1965).

In the experiment, children were exposed to aggressive and nonaggressive adult models and were observed in new situations in the absence of the model. The researchers predicted that participants exposed to aggressive models would reproduce aggressive acts resembling those of the models. The participants would differ in response both from participants who observed nonaggressive models and from those who had no prior exposure. The participants were boys and girls aged 3 to 5 years enrolled in a university-based nursery school. The study was based upon a formal experimental approach, one third being a control group, one third exposed to aggressive models and one third exposed to nonaggressive models. The impact of gender on the behaviours was tested by having equal numbers exposed to same-gender models and opposite-gender models. The control group had no prior exposure to the adult models and was tested only in the observation situation.

To increase the precision of the comparison between control and experimental group the children were rated for their aggressiveness before any trials began. Observers used four scales of displayed physical aggression, verbal aggression, aggression towards inanimate objects and aggressive inhibition. A composite score was obtained by summing the ratings on the four aggression scales; participants were rated independently by judges so as to permit an assessment of agreement. On the basis of the composite scores, the participants were arranged in triplets of equal ratings and assigned at random to one of two treatment conditions or to the control group.

Bandura and his team carried out many experiments and variations upon the experiments to identify the important factors and features of modelling, that is, copying the behaviour of others. In one set of experiments the participants were brought individually by the experimenter to the experimental room and were joined by the model. In the play area the experimenter demonstrated how the participant could design pictures with potato prints and picture stickers. These activities were selected since they had been established as having high interest value for the children.

After having settled the participant in one corner, the experimenter escorted the model to the opposite corner of the room that contained a small table and chair, a tinker toy set, a mallet and a 5-foot inflated Bobo doll. The experimenter explained to the model, within earshot of the participant, that these were the materials provided to play with, and after the model was seated, the experimenter left the experimental room. If the participant was to be exposed to aggression, the model would be aggressive towards the Bobo doll. With participants in the nonaggressive group, the model assembled the tinker toys in a quiet, subdued manner, totally ignoring the Bobo doll. The control group did not have this experience in the experimental room.

With participants who were to experience aggression, the model began by assembling the tinker toys but after approximately a minute had elapsed, the model turned to the Bobo doll and spent the remainder of the period being aggressive towards it. In particular, the model carried out highly idiosyncratic sequences of acts and spoken phrases, such as 'Sock him in the nose', 'Hit him down', 'Throw him in the air', 'Kick him', 'Pow' and 'Sockeroo', that would not be a natural part of the child's behaviour if they were not imitating the model. The participants were provided with a diverting task of toys on their play table that occupied their attention while at the same time ensured they could see the model's behaviour.

After 10 minutes, the experimenter re-entered the room and informed the participant that he/she would now go to another game room; they said goodbye to the model. In the new game room there were aggressive and nonaggressive toys laid out for the participant to play with. The experimenter sat discreetly away from the participant and the toys, which included:

- a 3-foot Bobo doll
- a mallet and peg board
- two dart guns
- a tether-ball with a face painted on it which hung from the ceiling
- a tea set
- crayons and colouring paper
- a ball
- two dolls
- three bears
- cars and trucks, and
- plastic farm animals.

The participant spent 20 minutes with these toys during which time his/her behaviour was rated in terms of predetermined response categories by judges who observed the session through a one-way mirror. Three measures of imitative behaviour were obtained:

1 physical, for example, striking the Bobo doll;
2 aggressive verbal; and
3 nonaggressive verbal, in which the participant repeats one of the model's phrases.

Non-imitative physical and verbal aggressive responses were also scored, including punching, slapping or pushing the doll and aggressive gun play. Ratings were also made of time the participants played nonaggressively or sat quietly and did not play with any of the toys at all.

The results when analysed confirmed that exposure of participants to aggressive models increases the probability of aggressive behaviour; their scores were significantly higher than those of either the nonaggressive or control groups, which did not differ from each other. However, with respect to the male model, the differences between the nonaggressive and control groups are striking; participants exposed to the nonaggressive male model performed significantly less physical and verbal aggression, and less mallet aggression, and they were less inclined to punch the Bobo doll. The hypothesis that boys are more prone than girls to imitate aggression exhibited by a model was only partially confirmed. The boys reproduced more imitative physical aggression than girls but there was no gender difference with regard to verbal aggression. Bandura carried out a large number of variations on the study, for example, the model was rewarded or punished in a variety of ways, the participants were rewarded for their imitations, the model was changed to be less attractive or less prestigious, and so on. This research revealed the imitative nature of humans and that modelling can be the source of new and modified behaviours.

Studies of behaviour continue but now those studies can be enhanced through the use of sophisticated technologies. The skilled and perfected performances of athletes, sports people, airline pilots, astronauts, surgeons and analysts require particularly demanding teaching regimes. Recent research by Andrew Mattar and Paul Gribble (2005) shows that the learning of complex behaviours can be explained with models that relate more to those of Pavlov, Skinner and Bandura than to the more recent explanations of the constructivist and social constructivists. 'They show that learning complex motor behaviours like riding a bicycle or swinging a golf club is based on acquiring neural representations of the mechanical requirements of movement' (Mattar and Gribble, 2005: 153). Those patterns of neurons serve two purposes – they hold the memory of the visual stimulus and they also hold the precept of the physical response. For example, coordinating muscle forces to control the club finds its origins in the learner observing and then copying the actions of the teacher. This is the neurological explanation of the value of modelling and shaping. Of course, the radical behaviourists reject such mentalistic explanations, but the modern behaviourist embraces the evidence while retaining the principle that the evidence and value of learning arise from the changes in behaviour and response. Mattar and Gribble's study provides evidence that mechanisms matching observation and action facilitate motor learning. 'Subjects who observed a video depicting another person learning to reach in a novel mechanical environment (imposed by a robot arm) performed better when later tested in the same environment than subjects who observed similar movements but no learning' (Mattar and Gribble, 2005: 153). They show that the effect is not based on conscious strategies but is dependent upon the implicit engagement of neural systems for movement planning and control.

Behaviour modification under scrutiny

Behaviourist approaches have proved particularly successful in areas of special educational needs. One area that has utilised behaviour modification and the use of reinforcement techniques to good effect is the education of autistic children.

Autism is a psychological condition with a wide range of symptoms which are commonly grouped under the triad of communication and speech; social interaction; and behaviour including restricted interests, repetitive behaviour, aggression and self-injury. Autism occurs in early childhood and has a poor prognosis; medical and cognitive therapies have not proved successful. Behaviour modification is seen to be a way of supporting autistic children and enabling them to make educational and social progress.

In this research (Lovaas, 1987), a group of 40 children were ranged based on learning ability; nearly half were considered normal, 10 per cent had severe learning difficulties and the rest had some learning difficulties. There was a control group of 19 autistic children. The participants of the experiment were assigned to one of two groups – the experimental group receiving the behaviour modification experience of clear instruction and reward for appropriate responses, and the control group receiving minimal treatment but acted to determine the rate of spontaneous improvement in children with autism. The allocation of children to experimental and control groups was based on convenience, but checks were made to ensure that there was not a bias that could affect the results. Pre-treatment assessments were based on a number of scales in use in the establishment: Bayley Scales of Infant Development (Bayley, 1955), the Cattell Infant Intelligence Scale (Cattell, 1960), the Stanford-Binet Intelligence Scale (Thorndike, 1972) and the Gesell Infant Development Scale (Gesell, 1949). There were also interviews with parents and behavioural observations based on video recordings of the participants' free-play behaviour in a playroom equipped with several simple early-childhood toys. The behaviours were scored in three ways – self-stimulatory (for example, repetitive behaviours), appropriate play and recognisable word utterances. There were double-blind checks on many of these judgements (Lovaas et al., 1973).

Post-treatment measures included collecting information about the participants' first-grade placement, intelligence, results from a repeat of the pre-treatment tests and assessment using the Wechsler Intelligence Scale for Children-Revised (WISC-R) (Wechsler, 1974), the Peabody Picture Vocabulary Test (Dunn, 1981) and the Merrill-Palmer Pre-School Performance Test (Stutsman, 1948).

The behaviour modification procedures were extensive, being an average of 40 hours per week for 2 or more years. The parents worked as part of the treatment team throughout the intervention; they were extensively trained in the treatment procedures so that treatment could take place for almost all of the participants' waking hours, 365 days a year. A detailed presentation of the treatment procedure has been presented in a teaching manual (Lovaas et al., 1980).

> The conceptual basis of the treatment was reinforcement (operant) theory; treatment relied heavily on discrimination-learning data and methods. Various behavioral deficiencies were targeted, and separate programs were designed to accelerate development for each behavior. High rates of aggressive and self-stimulatory behaviors were reduced by being ignored; by the use of time-out; by the shaping of alternate, more socially acceptable forms of behavior; and (as a last resort) by delivery of a loud 'no' or a slap on the thigh contingent upon the presence of the undesirable behavior. (Lovaas, 1987:5)

The results of the experiment are presented statistically with pre-treatment comparisons showing with a high reliability the equivalence of the control and experimental groups. 'The numbers of favorable versus unfavorable prognostic signs (directions of differences) on the pretreatment variables divide themselves equally between the groups. In short, the two groups appear to have been comparable at intake' (Lovaas, 1987: 7).

The follow-up analysis of the participants' performances indicated the strong progress made by the experimental group. In the IQ tests and placement in the schooling system, at intake, there were no significant differences, but at follow-up, the experimental group was significantly higher than the control group on educational placement and IQ test performance. In contrast, the control participants remained virtually unchanged between intake and follow-up, consistent with findings from other studies (Freeman *et al.*, 1985; Rutter, 1970). The introduction of a contingent aversive to four participants of the experimental and control groups, 'a shout "No" or a slap on the thigh … resulted in a sudden and stable reduction in the inappropriate behaviors and a sudden and stable increase in appropriate behaviors' (Lovaas, 1987: 10). This research illustrates the application of behaviourist principles and the rigorous analysis of their impact.

Providing models for behaviour

The next examples are drawn from current publications and illustrate the diverse areas in which research focusing upon behaviourist approaches takes place. With each example there is a challenge for the reader to identify how similar principles of practice and theory would apply in their teaching situations, albeit very different. The challenge to teachers is to identify strategies of teaching and imaginatively apply them to their situation. The examples include using video and using virtual reality to promote appropriate learning, dealing with the way pupils behave in class and reflecting upon the behaviour of teachers and the impact upon learning.

There is much debate in the media about the appropriateness of role models for young people. Adolescents in particular are vulnerable; they are in a time of identity formation and they are very exposed to the media where there is a great deal of attention given to the inappropriate behaviours of celebrities. The impact of modern technologies means that the slightest indiscretions of the role model are immediately and widely broadcast before the situation can be remediated. The 'bad' story is disseminated, and before a more positive response can be made, the next 'bad' story overtakes the previous. The perceived impact of the media upon the behaviour of young people reflects the same principles as those arising from Bandura's Bobo the Clown studies. These next research examples show how positive role models can have an influence upon the behaviour of the learners.

The first study (Paterson and Arco, 2007: 660) examines the effects of video modelling. The participants of the study were boys with autism; a characteristic of autism is repetitive actions. The study identified the impact upon the repetitive activities and the development of more appropriate play behaviours. Video modelling produced increases in appropriate play and decreases in repetitive play. Other reports of studies, for example, Rayner, Denholm and Sigafoos (2009), identify a range of affordances of video as the model for learners. There is an important debate regarding whether video images of 'self' are more effective than similar images of 'other' and the compromise of using the camera with an 'other' model but filmed from the position of the eyes, thus helping the learner to experience what they would see. One study (Charlop-Christy, Le and Freeman, 2000) showed the efficacy of video was better than that of live modelling and also reflects upon the positive resource costs of video over real experience. Each participant was presented with two similar tasks from his or her curriculum; one task was used for the video condition, while the other was used for the in vivo condition. Video modelling consisted of each child watching a videotape of models performing the target behaviour, whereas in vivo modelling consisted of the participant observing live models perform the target behaviour. After the observations, children were tested for acquisition and generalisation of the target behaviours. An important observation is that the appropriate play did not generalise from zero levels but there was the basis of 'appropriate' behaviour in their repertoires. When we consider the practical issues of supporting adolescent learners, we can provide the appropriate situations that give good role models, but we also have to ensure that the adolescents also possess the necessary skills and carry out the appropriate behaviours. We have to consider how the adolescents identify those appropriate behaviours.

We often require our learners to present their ideas to the rest of the class. We feel that it is an important skill to be able to stand up in front of others and, with confidence, speak. It is an important element of learning that the concept can be articulated. Some pupils and many adults find the situation daunting, and the difficulties adults experience is recognised as public speaking anxiety. This next piece of research (Wallach, Safir and Bar-Zvi, 2009) shows how, by changing the context, the appropriate skills can be developed by the learner, and they can be more readily supported by the mentor or teacher. The difficulty associated with supporting children with this anxiety is that the context makes the exposition by the learner the focus, and any intervention by the teacher relating to the anxiety would interfere with the flow and content of the exposition. It would also draw to the attention of the other pupils the anxiety of the presenter. The same is true in an adult situation where the public speaking context is not accessible by a mentor and if it was, any intervention might disclose the anxiety issue to the audience. In the study, the experimental group receives the modelling stimulus by means of a virtual reality headset giving a 3D stereoscopic view. The headset has a virtual orientation tracking system which detects the different movements of pitch, roll and yaw of the head. The learner's visual experience reflects that of their head movement as they look up, down or around or if they turn their head to the side. It provides scenes in which the participant is required to read from their text that appears on a podium in the virtual world in front of a large audience in various situations. The mentor controls the situation according to the stage in the learner's experience. The response of the audience can be made to be positive (for example, clapping), negative (for example, hostile remarks) or supportive (for example, asking questions). The mentor is in direct control of the situation, and the learner can be introduced to more challenging situations at an appropriate point in their training. Current research at the University of Southampton is investigating the viability of using the 3D multi-user virtual environment (MUVE) of Second Life (available online at http://secondlife.com) in which medical students experience talking to and asking questions of a patient. The patients' responses are driven by an expert system. In this situation, the students' understanding of the diagnostic concepts and their knowledge of medical conditions can be practised without the tensions or potential hazards of diagnosing real patients. This system has the advantage over the previously described mentor-controlled system in that, once set up, the learners can choose when and where to use the learning environment, and repeating the process has no extra cost in terms of resource or mentor time.

The next source of research evidence relates to the physical posture of learners. The study (Noda and Tanaka-Matsumi, 2009) evaluates the effect of a classroom-based behavioural intervention package to improve Japanese elementary school children's sitting posture in regular classrooms. As teachers, we know that creating the right context for learning is important. In some situations the learning processes are negatively impacted upon by factors that are not directly connected to the curriculum, teaching materials or actions of the teacher – these include the dress (attire) of the learners, interpersonal relationships, the quality of the décor, the location of the teaching area, distracting elements immediately outside the teaching area, etc. The posture of the learners is one of those factors. A class of slouching, dishevelled and apparently disorganised and disinterested adolescents is perceived to be a very different teaching challenge to that of a group of attentive learners. The signs of attentiveness are sitting and facing the teacher, positive eye contact and little off-task, interpersonal communication. This study investigates the efforts to modify the pupils' behaviour in order to improve their preparedness for learning. Appropriate sitting posture is described with four components: feet, buttocks, back and a whole body, that is, both feet are flat on the floor, buttocks are in contact with the chair seat, the learner's back is straight up and their body is facing forwards. The teachers and assistants were trained to recognise all four components of good posture. Two pre-intervention checks were made to establish that the level of poor posture was consistent. All four aspects of posture had to be satisfied to meet the standard of appropriate posture. The conclusions of the study relate to the effectiveness of group activities to improve the children's sitting posture. Teaching specific behavioural components of good posture, practising them and providing students with positive feedback and reinforcement are approaches teachers can use in their classrooms.

Noda's work was carried out with 7 and 8 year olds in two conventional classrooms with approximately 35 children in each class. The data on 68 children were recorded. A baseline of pupil behaviour was established showing only 20 per cent of the pupils adopted appropriate postures in both classes before the intervention. This figure rose to 90 per cent as a result of the intervention. A small number of children who were excluded from the data were given modified interventions with raised levels of support and reinforcement to enable them to adopt appropriate posture. The intervention package includes modelling of the appropriate behaviour by the teacher and correspondence training where the appropriate relationship (correspondence) between what the person says and what he or she does is reinforced. The researchers identify this area as one where further investigation is needed to examine whether the correspondence training promotes generalisation in group training. 'In the future, teachers may be trained to adapt aspects of correspondence training in the form of cue words, for example, to encourage appropriate posture acquired in training. Generalisation programming remains to be an important agenda for future research' (Noda and Tanaka-Matsumi,

2009: 272–3). A further observation arising from this study is that the change in behaviour is accompanied by a change in academic performance. This is in line with others (Doane, 1959; Whitman *et al.*, 1982), both showing that there is a direct and positive relationship between sitting posture and academic performance.

It can be argued that the improvement in academic performance does not arise from the change in posture but is simply a result of the attention given by the teacher to the pupils, making the pupils more responsive to all aspects of the teacher's interventions and so giving an all-round increase in performance. The 'Hawthorne effect' was the increased rate or quality of performance that was noted even in apparently adverse conditions when a group is subjected to observation. The term was coined by Henry Landsberger when carrying out studies for Western Electric Company at its Hawthorne plant in Chicago (Landsberger, 1958). It is possible in this study that such an effect is taking place. However, if the outcome of any intervention is positive with regard to the aims of education, then it can be argued that it is not important whether it is a direct or indirect effect of the intervention.

A final note regarding the research by Noda is that '[t]eachers' acceptance of the intervention program proved to be excellent' (Noda, 2008: 263). The researchers also assessed the teacher acceptability of the intervention as an index of the programme's social validity. They adopted six relevant items from Witt and Martens' (1983) questionnaire to assess the acceptability of the intervention. The most important negative aspect of the intervention was the amount of teacher time consumed by the intervention. A lot of time was needed to understand and carry out the procedures in the posture improvement project. However, there was a maximum score given by the teachers to the overall impact of the intervention on the children.

Self-management in behaviour change

The next example of the application of behaviourist approaches focuses upon the modification of behaviours exhibited by a minority of pupils. Three adolescents recognised as having ADHD (attention–deficit and hyperactivity disorder) were taught using methods focusing upon positive reinforcement of appropriate behaviour and the promotion of self-management procedures. The research shows how they have been used in school settings to successfully reduce problem behaviours, as well as to reinforce appropriate behaviour. The behaviour change is intended to make the learners more ready for learning by focusing their attention on preparation and organisation.

The study (Gureasko-Moore, DuPaul and White, 2006) began with a baseline activity to determine the level and nature of the behaviours of the learners but was measured with the preferred outcomes in mind. The areas focused on were being seated when the bell rang; making eye contact with the teacher; stopping other activities when the teacher is giving instructions; having a pen/pencil, notebook, paper and textbook ready on the desk; handing in homework when requested; and completing each item of the homework. The participants of the study were selected on the basis of teachers' reports suggesting that the students were insufficiently prepared for class and inconsistently completing assignments. The intervention involved introducing self-management procedures that focus on the improvement of learning preparedness. The first stage is to introduce the students to the strategies of self-management, including problem identification, goal setting, self-monitoring, self-evaluation and self-reinforcement. These training sessions took place in private at a time when the student would normally be doing school work. The second aspect of the intervention is the monitoring of the students' use of their newly acquired skills of classroom preparation during academic classes.

The self-management training is necessarily structured to introduce the strategies in a logical and supportive way. It begins with an explanation and rationale for self-management including a description of their current classroom behaviour. An important aspect of the behaviourist approach is that reward for progress should be given; to establish if progress has taken place then a baseline of performance must be established. By establishing that baseline before intervention, the progress from that point can be part of the contract between teacher and learner. The next stage was to give an explanation of the importance of responsibility for one's own behaviour; this is a critical aspect of self-management. Other behaviourist approaches based upon operant conditioning attempt to override the motivations of the learner and modify their behaviour without their conscious participation.

> Baseline is the measure of typical behaviour before any intervention is applied.

In self-management techniques, the value is in the learner's proactive participation in the behaviour change. In this study the 'self-management plan was taught to the students to be used specifically in their targeted academic classroom. The students were instructed to begin self-managing their behaviour on the second day of the training phase. The students were provided with two forms of the self-management plan: (a) the student log and (b) the self-monitoring checklist' (Gureasko-Moore, DuPaul and White, 2006: 168). The student log is an important part of the self-management intervention because they can feel that they have ownership of the situation and the method by which their progress will be measured. The self-monitoring checklist is part of the contract between teacher and learner. In this study, the content was predetermined by the teacher (researcher) but in many interventions, the negotiation between learner and teacher is part of the self-management process.

The study revealed a pattern of behaviour change that is typical of behaviourist interventions showing the baseline levels, increases in appropriate behaviours during the interventions, a degree of fading but also a level of maintenance of the desired behaviours after the intervention. (See Figure 1.2, p. 5.) The study determined that the self-management intervention produced positive effects with increased preparedness for learning in the classroom. It is interesting to reflect upon the limitations of the conclusions. The students were recognised to have ADHD, which places them at the more severe aspect of the spectrum of classroom behaviours associated with failing to be ready for learning. The impact of a successful approach will be more readily seen when used in more severe circumstances than when used in more normal circumstances. In addition, there are different forms of inappropriate behaviour associated with preparedness to learn, those that seek attention and the more impulsive and unpredictable behaviours associated with hyperactivity. Separating the impact of the strategies upon those different behaviours is difficult when dealing with real people exhibiting both sorts of behaviour in different proportions.

Obviously, this study does not determine the efficacy of using such methods with pupils with less-demanding behaviours, but the education of 'normal' classes of adolescents is often characterised by less severe forms of similar behaviours, and it is possible that similar techniques to establish creative and effective learning environments would prove successful. The behaviourist teacher seeks to establish learning by ensuring that the learners' behaviours are conducive to learning; the behaviourist teacher is ensuring that the learners exhibit in their behaviour preparedness to learn.

The impact of reward and praise

Finally, in this chapter that outlines some aspects of the research relating to behaviourist approaches to learning, we look to the behaviour of the teacher and reflect upon the impact that it has on the learners' behaviours and the learning that is taking place in the classroom. We will consider the impact of the teachers' approval and disapproval taking place during classroom activities in four studies (Darch and Gersten, 1985; Thomas *et al.*, 1978; White, 1975; Wyatt and Hawkins, 1987).

Mary White's work (1975) with 104 teachers questions whether the challenges experienced by some teachers such as lack of learner interest and poor learner concentration and motivation could be more effectively dealt with by deeper analysis of the approval/disapproval teacher behaviours. She noted that disapproval dominated over approval from the middle years (pupils aged 9 years and over). John Thomas' study (1978) examined the approval and disapproval rates of ten teachers over 40 hours of observation.

They specified the learners' behaviours they would expect responses by the teacher to occur:

- putting hand up to say something;
- listening when the teacher is talking;
- working quietly at their desk;
- asking the teacher if they want to leave their desk;
- moving quietly about the room; and
- finishing the set work and moving on to the extra work.

Off-task behaviours that they expected teachers' disapproval responses for were noise (calling out, talking, singing, whistling, screaming, yelling); inappropriate movement (leaving desk without permission, banging classroom furniture, fighting, jumping out window); and staring away from the focus of the lesson. The results showed very similar rates of teacher approval and disapproval responses to the learners even though there were wide differences in the contexts of the teaching.

The Darch and Gersten (1985) study of reading development showed that on-task behaviour and reading accuracy was increased with social praise given by the teacher although the focus of this study was the rate of stimulus and response and its impact upon learning. In the Wyatt and Hawkins study (1987), existing rates of teacher approval and disapproval were assessed over the full range of ages of teaching from early years (4–8 year olds), secondary (14 year olds) and post-compulsory (16 year olds) in a variety of lessons and teaching contexts. Teachers' mean rates of both approval and disapproval tended to be highest with younger learners and lower with older pupils. The results were generally in line with those reported by White (1975) but the Wyatt and Hawkins study did question whether learner disillusionment was caused by the dominance of the disapproval with the older learners. With the teachers in the study, approval and disapproval rates were not related to their ages, years of experience or recency of training. They did conclude that teacher training should focus more on the skills of giving appropriate verbal approval and that this could, in particular, support classroom management.

Summary

In this chapter the major research of some key behaviourists has been examined including:

- the rote learning investigations;
- research on social modelling;
- the relevance of research with animals; and
- scrutiny of intense programmes of behaviour modification;

and three areas of research relating to classroom practice have been described:

1 providing models for behaviour;
2 self-management in behaviour change; and
3 the impact of reward and praise.

In the next chapter the theories arising from the research and practice of behaviourists over the previous century will be described and their relevance to classroom practice identified. Chapter 4 will then describe the pedagogic practices that have arisen and are successfully supporting teaching and learning.

Activities

- Consider, in the light of the content of the chapter, the different areas in which behaviourist ideas have been researched.
- Compare the different approaches to research.
- Consider how the research might support particular teaching strategies.

3
Theory

By the end of this chapter you will be:

- able to recall the important theories of behaviourism;
- able to describe the development of theories from the classical through operant to the social;
- aware of the emphasis on the positive aspects of behaviour change; and
- aware of the role of negative reinforcement.

In schools today we are under pressures from different directions, most with the same aim of increasing learning but some having a differing impact. Teachers are under pressure arising from the need to justify their current position (for example, peer appraisal and performance management procedures); the need to make professional progress (evidencing threshold standards of performance); the requirements arising from increased adherence to codes of conduct; the workload of an increased and changing prescription of the curriculum; the additional tasks from an increasing bureaucracy of rules and regulation; the tensions arising from public scrutiny of performance (through examination results and league tables); the challenges of changing mores of learner attitudes to both education and each other; the challenges of changing mores of learner behaviours; the demands of changing expectations of the learners in terms of teaching methods and resources; and the increasing complexity of classroom resourcing, in particular the technology associated with administration as well as teaching. This chapter will outline the theories associated with learning and behaviourism and make direct reference to these environmental, personal and behavioural aspects of teaching.

Behaviourism offers teachers the power to determine the pre-conditions for learning by impacting upon the preparedness of learners for the learning experience, to make more efficient methods of learning through behaviourist procedures of repetition, reinforcement, shaping and modelling and to make the curriculum more accessible through task analysis and sequencing. In this chapter, the emerging theories of behaviourism are described.

A theory is an unproven conjecture or hypothesis that gives a tentative insight into a complex situation through to a well-substantiated explanation of that complex situation. A theory can be a coherent set of statements or a logical structure that attempts to explain or represent observed phenomena in the form of facts, observations or events. Those statements of the expectation of what should happen, barring unforeseen circumstances, can be used to predict what might happen. A theory can never be established beyond all doubt. It is in that light that the theories and postulates of the major psychologists are presented.

The theorists that have important statements to make about education begin with Pavlov and Watson and their work on animals that Pavlov extended to explain human behaviour. By the 1920s Watson had left academic psychology, and other behaviourists were becoming influential, proposing new forms of learning other than classical conditioning. Skinner's theory of operant conditioning followed upon Thorndike's work with animals and his laws of conditioning. Skinner acknowledged the processes of the mind but considered it simply more productive to study observable behaviour rather than pontificate about internal mental events. He concentrated on the causes of an action and its consequences, coined the phrase 'operant conditioning' and described the processes and applications of behaviour modification. Albert Bandura is the link between the behaviourist focus upon behaviour and the cognitive discourse on mental processes (1969).

Classical conditioning

Ivan Pavlov, the Russian physiologist, carried out Nobel Prize-winning work in the field of digestion. One particular study involved collecting the saliva from dogs as they were restrained in an experimental chamber. Tubes were surgically implanted into the saliva glands so that when food was shown to the dogs, the saliva could be collected for study. Pavlov noticed that the saliva sometimes appeared before the dog saw the meat, and he made the connection that the dog anticipated the arrival of the meat by perhaps the clicking of the mechanism for dispensing the food or the arrival of the experimenter. He called the phenomenon psychic reflex. Pavlov then experimented by making the delivery of the food coincident with another stimuli, the ringing of a bell being most commonly stated. Before the experiment the ringing of the bell did not cause salivation; it, in those circumstances, is a neutral stimulus. During the conditioning phase, the bell becomes associated with the arrival of food and the dogs salivate. After conditioning, when the bell is rung, even without the presence of food, the dogs salivate. This association between a neutral stimulus and a response is called classical conditioning. Pavlov dedicated much of the rest of his life to extending these findings and extrapolating them to the human condition (Pavlov, 1927). He studied similar reflexes, the automatic behaviour that is caused by a stimulus from the environment. For example, the blinking of the eye is a reflex reaction in response to a visual or physical movement near the eye, as is a baby's suckling movement when something is placed in their mouth. His theories focus on observable behaviour and the manipulation or conditioning of those reflex actions, arguing that behaviour can be measured and thought cannot; evidence is the keyword in his theorising. In his work, it can be considered that the human mind is a 'black box' that cannot be opened. It is only what goes into the box and what comes out of the box that can be known and reported with scientific rigour. This is an underpinning principle of the behaviourist movement in psychology.

Before conditioning there is no response to the conditioned stimulus.

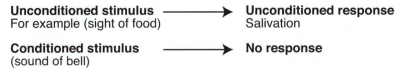

Conditioning takes place when the conditioned stimulus is made to occur simultaneously with the unconditioned stimulus.

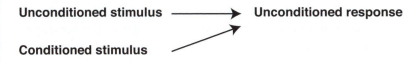

After conditioning the conditioned stimulus causes the conditioned response.

Figure 3.1 The process of classical conditioning

Figure 3.1 illustrates the process of classical conditioning. Before the conditioning the sight of food and the salivation are unconditioned stimulus and unconditioned response, respectively. During the conditioning phase a neutral stimulus is introduced that is coincidental with the unconditioned stimulus. In the final stage, after the neutral stimulus has become the conditioned stimulus, the response is also conditioned and will occur without the original unconditioned stimulus.

Stimulus, response and consequence

Edward Thorndike summarised his findings in a set of 'laws'. These are extensive and diverse in the degree of importance and the impact upon pedagogy arising from them. The basis of Thorndike's approach to problems of behaviour lies in the belief that human behaviour can be analysed and studied in terms of stimulus–response and measures of the strength, endurance and re-establishment of the stimulus–response connection. Learning is the establishment of the bond between stimulus and response, and humans only differ from other animals in their greater capacity to make the connections between their response and the consequences. The first principle he developed suggests those responses to a situation that are closely followed by satisfaction will become firmly attached and therefore more likely to reoccur when the situation is repeated. This is the underpinning thesis of operant conditioning upon which Skinner developed much of his work. Conversely, if the situation is followed by discomfort, the connections to the situation will become weaker, and the behaviour or response is less likely to occur when the situation is repeated. The law of effect states that the likely recurrence of a response is generally determined by its consequence or impact upon the individual whether that is rewarding or punishing. A positive consequence strengthens reinforcement, whilst a negative response weakens reinforcement. An act which results in discomfort tends to be disassociated from the situation, so that when the situation recurs, the act will be less likely to recur. The greater the satisfaction or the greater the discomfort experienced, the greater the degree to which the stimulus–response association will be strengthened or weakened.

After further research studies Thorndike proposed the truncated law of effect that added the idea that while reward responses always strengthen the bond between a stimulus and a response, the effect of punishment responses is less predictable; sometimes they weaken the association, but sometimes they do not. A principled interpretation, which will be illustrated later, is 'we reward appropriate behaviour, we ignore inappropriate behaviour'. The degree to which we can ignore some behaviour in the classroom can rely

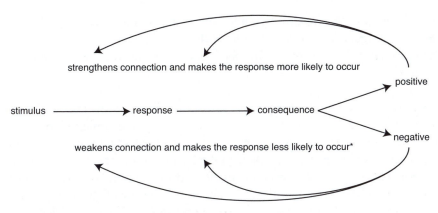

*See Thorndike's 'truncated law of effect' below.

Figure 3.2 Thorndike's laws of effect and repetition impact upon stimulus–response

significantly on our principled application of the approach.

Thorndike's law of exercise or repetition is précised as the more responses to the stimulus that are reinforced, the longer and the more sustained the connection will be. It is often said that 'practice makes perfect'. In a later revision of the law, Thorndike clarifies that repetition in itself does not make perfect, but practice that provides the learner with informed feedback about progress and performance could be valuable in strengthening the stimulus–response connection and thus increasing the frequency of response. We will see that this provides a rationale for formative assessment, assessment for learning and ipsative assessments based upon learners' prior attainment.

Thorndike's law of readiness asserts that, before learning takes place, the learner has to be ready to learn. That can be interpreted in terms of basic needs (making sure the learner is not hungry, thirsty, stressed, uncomfortable, etc.) or in terms of cognitive abilities such as an appropriate repertoire of responses, motivation to respond, sensitivity to the stimulus or readiness for action. Further, a series of stimulus–response connections can be chained together if they belong to the same action (reaction) sequence. One response causes the stimulus for the next, and the learning pattern is established because the learner is ready or prepared by having exercised the responses previously. This process of chaining is an important strategy for developing complex learning patterns.

The law of recency states that the most recently reinforced response is the one that is likely to determine the recurrence of a response to a particular stimulus. For example, during the previous weeks a pupil has responded differently to the challenge of adding two digits:

- taking counters, making two piles and counting the total;
- using fingers and counting on from the first digit; and
- drawing dominoes of the numbers and counting the total number of dots.

Each has received similar reward for correct answers, either intrinsically by the knowledge of being correct or extrinsically by the praise, smile, tick or token coming from the teacher. All being equal, the most recent reinforced response will make that response more likely in the future. In the real classroom, there is probably differentiated reinforcement, and one arithmetic method may receive more reinforcement than another and so the law of effect determines future responses. In other words, the method of carrying out a calculation will be the one that gives the right answer and therefore the one that gives the most immediate response, the intrinsic sense of success from getting the answer right. Other factors influencing that will be the response from the teacher or others in the classroom. Wesley Becker identifies four forms of social reinforcement: verbal, facial, proximity and touch (Becker *et al.*, 1967). The use of touch, and even proximity in some circumstances, is to be used with caution in the school environment. All four are identified as powerful reinforcers, and much use is made of verbal praise and visual approval (smiling, winking, laughing, nodding, etc.). Becker identifies a difference between judgemental praise such as *good*, *well done*, *cool* or *neat*, and evaluative praise where the teacher is seen to take the time to identify how or in what way the work is praiseworthy. In assessment for learning, it is giving feedback that clearly states both the progress being made and the attainments being achieved that best supports learning. Developing Becker's work, Donald MacMillan writes: 'Describe the behaviour and indicate that you appreciate it … you not only compliment the child but you carefully point out precisely what he has done to warrant the praise – hence it is educational' (1973: 182).

There are many subsidiary laws that have important implications for pedagogy and are noted here for completeness. Thorndike's law of primacy is interpreted as 'what is learned first is learned best'. The law of multiple responses suggests that if a response fails to produce satisfaction, another response will be triggered until success results and learning becomes possible, but complementary, the law of response analogy considers that a learner's response to a novel situation is determined by innate tendencies to respond. The law of response analogy also indicates that features in similar situations will encourage response if responses have been rewarded in the past. The law of set states the individual's total attitude or disposition affects response rates and thus learning.

Thorndike noticed in animal behaviour that they could become capable of ignoring some aspects of a problem and responding to others – thus the law of selectivity of response. The law of associative shifting applies when a learned pattern of response to a given stimulus is transferred, by association, to another stimulus. The law of spread effect indicates that each stimulus–response relationship is not an isolated event, but the association and reward mechanism can have an influence upon other actions that occur at the same time. Finally, the law of intensity relates to the vividness of the stimulus–response–consequence experience – the degree to which the process impacts upon the senses.

Operant conditioning and schedules of reinforcement

The research and writings of B. F. Skinner have determined to a large extent the course of behaviourism in education, beginning with his experiments with animals. Operant conditioning is the underpinning theory – behaviours occur but it is the behaviours that receive positive reinforcement or some form of tangible or intrinsic rewards that are repeated. That reward is also called the reinforcing stimulus, or reinforcer, and has the effect of increasing the operant behaviour. Skinner's basic principle of operant conditioning is that a response followed by a reinforcer is strengthened and is therefore more likely to occur again. The principles are:

- the reinforcer must follow the response;
- the reinforcer must follow immediately (timing is important);
- the reinforcer must be impactful (magnitude is important);
- the reinforcer must be consistent; and
- the reinforcer must be contingent on the response.

In the experiments, the obvious happened; when the reinforcer was removed, the behaviour reduced and eventually stopped (other than as part of random actions). This is called extinction and is described below. The important aspect of operant conditioning is that when the reinforcer is reintroduced, the resulting behaviour pattern is more quickly established. And this in turn forms the basis of schedules of reinforcement. Interestingly, Skinner himself rejected the idea of theories of learning in one of his earlier works (Skinner, 1950). Also, although analysing and rejecting forms of theorising, he does not deny other interpretations and explanations of learning. He writes, 'It is not the purpose of this paper to show that any of these theories cannot be put in good scientific order, or that the events to which they refer may not actually occur or be studied by appropriate sciences' (1950: 195). This

Behaviour is followed by a consequence, and the nature of the consequence modifies the tendency to repeat the behaviour in the future.

Behaviour followed by a reinforcing stimulus results in an increased probability of that behaviour occurring in the future (positive reinforcement).

Behaviour no longer followed by a reinforcing stimulus results in a decreased probability of that behaviour occurring in the future (extinction).

Figure 3.3 Operant conditioning

reinforces the idea that behaviourists do not and need not concern themselves with the mechanics (biological or biochemical) of learning but with the physical and verbal consequences of experience. Even so, the paper reveals how the study of simple behaviours in animals can give insight into such concepts as emotion.

In the simple operant conditioning situation (see Figure 1.1, p. 3) 'a pigeon learning to peck a disc when it appears and then receiving an edible reward', the response rates can be measured. The rate of response varies and can be enhanced by differential reinforcements. However, as the pigeon becomes less hungry there appears to be a change in the pattern of response. The pigeon can and does respond on occasions just as quickly but there is a higher level of latency of response.

By giving the bird more food, for example, we induce a condition in which it does not always respond. But the responses that occur show approximately the same temporal relation to the stimulus ... In extinction, of special interest here, there is a scattering of latencies because lack of reinforcement generates an emotional condition. Some responses occur sooner and others are delayed, but the commonest value remains unchanged. (Skinner, 1950: 196)

A classroom interpretation would be that a learner continues to respond to the lesson experiences but with increasing amounts of latency as the reward for response (whether physical, tokenised or intrinsic) diminishes.

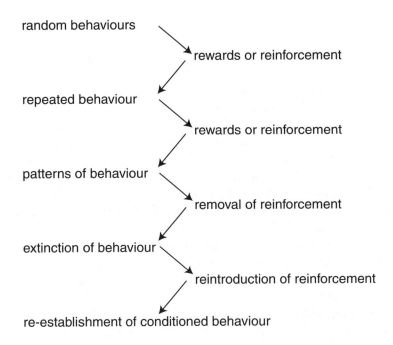

Figure 3.4 Steps to conditioning

Figure 3.4 shows the typical process of establishing or learning new behaviours or responses. The steps move from random behaviours being selected through positive reinforcement with rewards building to patterns of behaviour. In the absence of reinforcement, extinction of responses may occur. The reintroduction of reinforcement causes the return of the behaviour patterns. The way in which reinforcement is managed is called scheduling.

Skinner established that conditioning could be optimised through a pattern of repeated and reduced reinforcement of the desired behaviours and that schedules of reinforcement are important components of the learning process and impact on the strength and rate of the responses. Two types of reinforcement schedules are continuous reinforcement and partial reinforcement. In continuous reinforcement, the desired behaviour is reinforced every time it occurs. This schedule is best applied during the early stages of learning in order to establish a strong connection between the behaviour and the response. Once the connections have been made then it is more appropriate to move to the less resource-demanding partial reinforcement. However, reducing the rate or strength of reinforcement may lead to extinction. Interestingly, the research evidence produced by Skinner shows that partial reinforcement strengthens the stimulus–response condition and makes the behaviour less susceptible to extinction. That is, partial reinforcement is more effective than continuous reinforcement.

Partial reinforcement can be of several types, including fixed-ratio, variable-ratio, fixed-interval and variable-interval schedules. The fixed-ratio schedule gives reinforcement after every 'x' occurrences of the behaviour and reputedly gives the most highly sustained behaviour pattern with regard to the amount of reinforcement. Variable-ratio schedules provide reinforcement after an unpredictable number of responses – this is congruent with the busy activities of the classroom, creates a high steady rate of responding and avoids the reward-dependency of fixed and continuous reinforcement. The 'interval' of interval schedules refers to the time following the appropriate response before the reward is given. The fixed-interval schedule causes high amounts of responding near the end of the interval, but much slower responding immediately after the delivery of the reinforcer (Dews, 1978). The variable-interval schedules occur when a response is rewarded after an unpredictable amount of time has passed. This schedule produces a slow, steady rate of response.

David Premack devised a principle that helps identify appropriate and effective reinforcers. Premack's Principle states that any high probability behaviour will serve as a reinforcer for any low probability behaviour, and vice versa, a low probability behaviour will act as a punishment for a high probability behaviour (1959, 1971). For example, during break time pupils often go to the open access computers to surf the Web (a high probability behaviour); that activity can be used as a reward for doing a low probability behaviour such as completing a lesson-based task in a timely way. A high probability behaviour is playing in the sandpit; it can be used as a reward for the lower probability behaviour of listening to a story without interruption. In subsequent works, commentators have substituted the word probability with frequency and preference but both represent the same predilection of the learner to carry out particular tasks.

An important element of the behaviourist theories arising from Skinner's work relates to shaping. Shaping is a technique used by the teacher by which the learner is reinforced for showing closer and closer approximations to desired behaviour. It is an aspect of behaviour analysis that gradually teaches new behaviour through the use of reinforcement until the target behaviour is achieved (Skinner, 1953: 63; Staats, 1963: 76). Shaping is 'the process in which reinforcement is differentially applied to those responses that constitute a closer and closer approximation to the ultimate response one wishes to bring about' (Wenrich, 1970: 85). It is useful in teaching new desired behaviours that may be outside their normal experience or activities. For example, the learner may not have experienced 'hot seating', an activity where one person of the group is the focus of attention and that person both controls and responds to the questioning by the rest of the group. It is a complex scenario when met for the first time but through shaping – reinforcing prerequisite behaviours and skills – the learner can eventually play the full and proper role in the activity as either a class member or the person in the 'hot seat'. Shaping is a natural way of encouraging the learner to increase the prevalence of a clearly defined, desired behaviour because it does not overtly challenge the learner to do something new; shaping is most effective for increasing positive behaviour.

Extinction, in operant conditioning, is the reduction of reinforcement to reduce the occurrence of a behaviour. B. F. Skinner describes in his autobiography how he accidentally obtained his first extinction curve. A rat was pressing the lever in an experiment on satiation when the feeding mechanism jammed. Even though no food was being issued, the rat had continued to press the lever but after a little time the frequency of pressing reduced in a gradual curve. Skinner notes that 'the change was more orderly than the extinction of a salivary reflex in Pavlov's setting, and I was terribly excited. It was a Friday afternoon and there was no one in the laboratory whom I could tell. All that weekend I crossed streets with particular care and avoided all unnecessary risks to protect my discovery from loss through my accidental death' (Skinner, 1979: 95). Skinner goes on to report how he collected many more recordings with the same waveform of extinction. After the withdrawal of reinforcement there is an initial increase in the frequency of the behaviour followed by the steady decline.

Observational learning by modelling behaviour

People learn through observing others' behaviour, attitudes and the outcomes of those attitudes. 'Most human behavior is learned observationally through modeling: from observing others, one forms an idea of how new behaviors are performed, and on later occasions this coded information serves as a guide for action' (Bandura, 1997). People acquire behaviours through the observation of others, and they then imitate what they observe. Bandura recognises that much learning does take place as a result of reinforcement, but importantly, virtually all forms of behaviour can be learned in the absence of directly experienced reinforcement. 'Rather than experiencing reinforcement ourselves for each of our actions, we can learn through vicarious reinforcement by observing the behavior of others and the consequences of their behavior' (Schultz and Schultz, 2007). Observational learning is part of the social learning theory that explains human behaviour in terms of continuous reciprocal

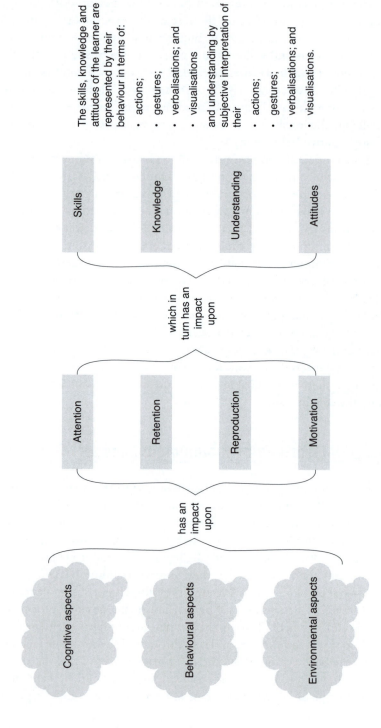

The skills, knowledge and attitudes of the learner are represented by their behaviour in terms of:

- actions;
- gestures;
- verbalisations; and
- visualisations

and understanding by subjective interpretation of their

- actions;
- gestures;
- verbalisations; and
- visualisations.

| Skills |
| Knowledge |
| Understanding |
| Attitudes |

which in turn has an impact upon

| Attention |
| Retention |
| Reproduction |
| Motivation |

has an impact upon

Cognitive aspects

Behavioural aspects

Environmental aspects

Figure 3.5 The processes of modelling

interaction between cognitive, behavioural and environmental influences. The process whereby new behaviours are learned is called modelling.

The necessary conditions for effective modelling can be summarised as attention, retention, reproduction and motivation. In other words, modelling will more readily occur when the learner's attention is assuredly drawn to the model, the learner remembers the pertinent aspects of the behaviour, ensuring the learner has the capabilities to reproduce the behaviours, and finally the learner is motivated.

The attention that a stimulus–response episode attracts is dependent upon many factors and has a number of features. Attention may originate from the three domains that Bandura identified – the environment, the behaviour of the model and the cognitive aspects. In general, behaviourists do not ponder deeply upon cognitive or mentalistic aspects of learning, but some aspects such as recognition, emotion, engagement, interest, memory, recall, etc. are so well represented by the external behaviours of the learner that the subjective perspectives are acknowledged as being useful. The environmental aspects that draw attention in the modelling process are most important, as they are the most controllable by the teacher in the classroom situation. The teacher has less control over the behavioural features of the model when that is other pupils or aspects of other pupils' behaviour. They are in more control when they are the model. The aspects of attention are:

- *sensual distinctiveness* – the impact is determined by how much the stimulus impacts upon the attention of the learner considering the physical senses of sight, hearing, touch, pain, smell, orientation, balance, position and taste;
- *affective distinctiveness* – the impact is determined by how much the stimulus impacts upon the attention of the learner considering the cognitive senses of fear, anxiety, pleasure, satisfaction, hatred and love;
- *prevalence* – the impact is determined by the frequency and duration of the stimulus–response episodes; and
- *functional value of the experience* – how much relevance there is to the individual concerned.

The retention factor is concerned with memory and recall. Bandura is the link between the behaviourist approaches to teaching and learning and the cognitive approaches to teaching and learning. In this area the behaviourist will not theorise upon the functioning of memory but is clear on the nature and patterns of recall or reproduction.

The reproduction factor is concerned with how readily the learner can reproduce the response to the stimulus. The effectiveness of a modelling strategy is therefore dependent upon the efficiency of that recall by the learner. Recall may take the form of symbolic representation, verbal description of mental images, drawing of mental images and verbal description of cognitive organisation, for example, 'I remember the numbers of days in each month by recalling a poem'. Recall is also demonstrated when the learner undertakes verbal rehearsal or motor rehearsal of the experience. Limiting factors include the physical capability to demonstrate or repeat the behaviour or response.

Motivation is a mentalistic feature that behaviourists accept as the power behind the operant conditioning process. The motivations to continue to display the same modelled behaviour can be based in the traditional behaviourist understanding of positive reinforcement, promised and therefore virtual rewards such as tokens and vicarious rewards (through seeing and recalling the reinforced model experienced by another).

The process of modelling, illustrated in Figure 3.5, identifies the three aspects that influence behaviour and by accepting the different influences upon behaviour the modern behaviourist can better explain, predict and determine the behaviour of the learners. Needless to say, the behaviourist makes no theory about those internal processes save but by the implications arising from observation of the learners' behaviours. Because of the close connections between the radical behaviourists' concepts of behaviour and the cognitive processes of personality, the social learning theory can be considered a bridge between behaviourist and cognitive learning theories.

Punishment, impact and alternatives

On the whole, behaviourists reflect little confidence in the effectiveness of punishment. There are also doubts about the efficacy of removing positive reinforcement. Punishment is not seen to be a solution, although it should be noted that it is a very widely used strategy in our schools. Although many people use it for short-term goals, its long-term objective is social control. Jena provides evidence for promoting 'development of internal control' (2008: 90).

'Punishment is a dead-end since its effects run straight into the teeth of major educational goals. If one gets a child to sit quietly or read because they are afraid not to do so, one is a long way from achieving the oft-stated goals of self-discipline and self-directed learning' (Hewett, 1968).

'The observation that nearly all antisocial adults have previously shown poor behaviour as children motivates the political will to empower public services, and in particular education, to promote social and emotional well-being of children and young people' (Robins, 1986: 227).

'Worse than not being fair to the learner who is, after all, doing what circumstances produced, punishment disrupts further progress. The harmful effects of punishment can be hard to eliminate' (Vargas, 2009: 178).

Thorndike's law of effect states that the likely recurrence of a response is generally determined by its consequence or impact upon the individual whether that is positive (rewarding) or negative (punishing). A negative response weakens reinforcement and makes the recurrence less likely.

The Premack Principle is a useful means by which teachers can determine whether a response will be a positive reinforcer or not. The principle, described earlier, states that low probability behaviour can act as a punishment (Premack, 1959, 1971). A punishment for the high probability behaviour of running in the corridor can be the low probability behaviour of sitting in silence in the school entrance. In a primary school setting, the punishment for a high probability behaviour of calling out during story time could be the low probability behaviour of sitting on a seat away from the rest of the group. The Premack Principle does not consider the efficacy of negative reinforcement or punishment in the sustained modification of behaviour or in creating the right environment for learning.

In Skinner's book *Walden Two* (1948), he describes a utopian society where human behaviour is scientifically controlled by a benign government. In this fictional account, he expresses his then thoughts and explicit claims that a science of human behaviour can reveal the means to control human behaviour. However, it is clear that there is no such overarching science that can be so deterministic of the individual will and that governmental, authoritarian, religious or political control of behaviour is limited. However, the role of positive reinforcement is explored, and the need to be cautious of any system of negative reinforcement (punishment) is considered. Providing that the rewards are appropriate, the evidence arising from the work of psychologists suggests that positive reinforcement changes behaviour, yet the evidence to the contrary is not as convincing. The operant conditioning terminology for discussing such factors is clear: positive reinforcement is a consequence that is rewarding; negative reinforcement is a consequence of an action that removes or reduces an aversive stimulus – this intervention is used in escape or active avoidance training. The rewarded behaviour 'results in the removal of the subject from that something, noting that either way, the effect is that the unpleasant something is no longer present' (Baucum, 1996: 113). When interpreting Thorndike's laws on conditioning, the second part of the law of effect implies positive punishment is one where a consequence is the introduction of an aversive stimulus; negative punishment is the removal of an appetitive stimulus (removing a reward). 'Negative punishment procedures such as time-out and response cost, which do not involve the application of aversive events, are much more acceptable and more commonly used than positive punishments' (Miltenberger, 2008: 421).

At the absolute level, the spectrum of activity that is the opposite to positive reinforcement stretches from the vicarious experience of someone else losing their positive reinforcement through to simulated drowning and near-death torture (Obama, 2009). It is within that spectrum (illustrated in Figure 3.6) that teaching and learning place reliance upon punishment to control behaviour and enable learning.

From the perspective of social behaviour theory, negative motivations exist; these provide reasons not to imitate someone. Like most traditional behaviourists, Bandura sees positive reinforcements as motivators, but unlike most radical behaviourists, he suggests that there are mechanisms of punishment that have a positive influence upon behaviour and learning. But like

punishment	exemplified	negative implication
vicarious experience of loss of positive reinforcement	seeing someone subject to a punishment (listed below)	loss of faith in the token system modelling of the inappropriate behaviour
threat of loss of positive reinforcement	removing the opportunity to earn tokens even when behaving appropriately	alienation against the teacher (contract broker)
	removal of previously earned tokens	alienation against the token economy
loss of positive reinforcement when behaving appropriately	removing the opportunity to earn tokens	alienation against the teacher (contract broker)
	removing earned tokens	alienation against the token economy
verbal chastisement	expressing disappointment, sorrow, embarrassment or anger because of the action	
	shouting, emotional criticism	alienation against the teacher (contract broker)
physical restraint	human direct force	teacher alienation
	within a locked room (cell)	no social engagement; less opportunity for positive reinforcement
	detention room	social engagement with similar others and thus reinforcement
	sent into isolation	loss of teacher control/supervision
	isolation within the classroom	focus of attention; perhaps rewarding
smacking	sharp tap to the leg	
	a hard slap on the leg	
corporal punishment	systematic swipes of a cane, slipper or hand	

Figure 3.6 Degrees of punishment

most traditional behaviourists, Bandura says that 'punishment in whatever form does not work as well as reinforcement and, in fact, has a tendency to backfire on us' (qtd. in Boeree, 2006: 5). His theories describe three aspects of punishment: previous experience of punishment; the promise of punishment (threat); and vicarious punishment. Vicarious punishment results in 'a decrease in the frequency of certain behaviors which occurs as a result of seeing others punished for the same actions (i.e. through observational learning)' (Ewen, 1993: 509). If an unwanted behaviour is punished, the rate of responding in that way to the stimulus (environment/opportunity) will be reduced but that reduction tends to be temporary. It is true that the effects of any reinforcement are only temporary, but intermittent reinforcing (see scheduling) can maintain higher rates of response more consistently than intermittent regimes of punishment can reduce the unwanted behaviour (Walters and Grusec, 1977).

Time-out is a technique that is currently promoted in television parenting programmes. It is an aversive and a form of punishment (MacMillan, 1973; Rogers, 2004) involving the forced removal of the learner from the environment where the inappropriate behaviours are being demonstrated to an environment that is non-stimulating for a period of time specified by the teacher. 'For this procedure to be effective two factors must be operating: first, the setting from which the child is removed must be reinforcing to, and desired by, the child; and second, the time-out environment must be neutral in stimulus value, or not desired' (MacMillan, 1973: 78–9). The implementation of a time-out policy requires consistent and reasonable rules for the teachers and a clear explanation of the process for the learners which answers the questions:

How do we remove the student from the class?
To whom and where?
How long should the student stay in time-out?
What happens when students refuse to leave the classroom?
What happens with the student during time-out?
On what basis do students negotiate entry back into the classroom?
(Rogers, 2004: 106).

One study of pupils with severe behavioural difficulties experimented with time-out periods of 1, 5, 10 and 20 minutes. The results did not support the use of extended periods of time-out, but suggested that a 5-minute duration was as or more effective than the other tested durations (McGuffin, 2006).

Bandura's work has extended into deeply psychological areas of behaviour management and has been successfully applied to the treatment of a number of conditions including phobias, lack of self-efficacy, repetitive behaviours and autism (Bandura, 1997). In some studies he worked with hyper-aggressive male adolescents who often had parents modelling hostile attitudes. He argues that antisocial aggression originates from the disruption of a child's dependency relationship on his parents. It is the lack of affectionate nurturance and close dependent ties to parents that means, without a model, there is no internalising standards of behaviour (Bandura and Walters, 1959, 1963). Although the parents would not tolerate aggression in the home, they would demand that their sons be tough and settle disputes with peers and, if necessary, do that through physical aggression. The parents would display aggression towards the school system, taking sides with their sons and even being aggressive towards other students in defence of their sons. The adolescents modelled the aggressive and hostile attitudes of their parents. This is explained that for the aggressive adolescents, 'the vicarious influence of seeing a model meting out punishment outweighed the suppressive effect of receiving punishment directly for aggressive acts' (Pajares, 2004). These findings are reflected in Bandura's books *Adolescent Aggression* (Bandura and Walters, 1959) and *Aggression: A Social Learning Analysis* (Bandura, 1973).

Commenting upon the way in which people fail to take control of their own environment, Bandura states that 'we find that people's beliefs about their efficacy affect the sorts of choices they make in very significant ways. In particular, it affects their levels of motivation and perseverance in the face of obstacles. Most success requires persistent effort, so low self-efficacy becomes a self-limiting process. In order to succeed, people need a sense of self-efficacy, strung together with resilience to meet the inevitable obstacles and inequities of life' (qtd. in Pajares, 2004).

A key theory arising from this work is called reciprocal determinism, and this sets Bandura aside from the radical behaviourists because of the cognitive step of interpreting the way in which the environment is perceived and impacts upon behaviour. Reciprocal determinism is the interaction of cognition, environmental events and behaviour that creates the human experience. Although learners' behaviour is largely shaped by their environment, their behaviour can affect the environment, which in turn can affect their cognition or interpretation of the environment, which in turn re-affects their behaviour.

Verbal behaviour and dealing with language

An important consideration when estimating the influence, interpretation and application of behaviourist principles relates to language. Critics of behaviourism (see Chapter 1) claim that behaviourism does not deal with language and the place of language in learning. This is far from the truth, but their misjudgement is perhaps understandable because language is a very special behaviour. Language is almost exclusively found in human beings, and it is an extremely small percentage of human beings that do not possess very powerful skills of language and expression. Language is also the behaviour most closely associated with our expression of learning and so holds an important place in any aspect of epistemology. But language is behaviour, and in the examples of operant conditioning already mentioned, from Bobo the Clown (Bandura, Ross and Ross, 1961) through to supporting people's presentational skills (Wallach, Safir and Bar-Zvi, 2009), language has been an important response to stimulus. Skinner's radical behaviourism did not accept the value of mentalistic processes in trying to understand the mechanism of learning. It is therefore better to define language from the behaviourist point of view as 'communication' – the outward expression of any mentalistic processes.

Bandura sees language as being a 'highly intricate response system' (1969: 138). He describes the difficulties some people have because the observational modelling of behaviour is dependent upon its discriminability. Learning the intricacies of oral language structures benefits from the verbal modelling cues being supplemented with technique that draws attention to the structure of syntax (Bandura, 1969: 138). He draws particular attention to the unique nature of language acquisition through modelling and the interrelationship between the learner and teacher (child and parent) in many studies (Bandura, 1969: 148–52).

Ullin Place argues for a 'linguistic behaviourism' (2004: 165) that keeps true to the scientific nature of Skinner's radical behaviourism with a philo-sophical connection between language and the environmental reality it represents. Within this social behaviour theory, Place recognises the greater importance of the verbal stimuli (the speaker) and the value of the sentence (not word) in influencing the behaviour of the listener. Although Place accepts Chomsky's (1957) ideas of a rules-based interpretation (construing and constructing) of speech, he insists that language is acquired 'by the same process of contingency shaping (error correction) as is observed in the acquisition of motor skills' (Place, 2004: 166). The implication is that verbal discourse is subject to operant conditioning, and verbal response can be understood in similar terms as physical responses are analysed. The classroom-based reinforcement of the verbalisation of knowledge, understanding and attitudes can influence knowledge, understanding and attitudes.

William Baum offers a definition of communication as 'when the behavior of one organism generates stimuli that affect the behavior of another organism' (2005: 130). He cites the alarm call of a single bird affecting the behaviour of the rest of the flock as being an example of communication but goes on to define communication as 'making common' between one person and another.

The alarm call of the bird is very different from the spoken message of a human – the former triggers a fixed pattern of behaviour dependent only upon the precedents and not the consequences. Whereas, the spoken word, because of the nature of the operant behaviour, will stimulate responses based both on the precedents and upon the consequences of the response. Baum's 'making common' of something may in fact evoke different responses from different people based upon the prior experience and conditioning of the individual.

In conclusion, the pre-radical behaviourists' views about language have been surpassed by the radicals' viewpoint that language is like any other behaviour and so can be stimulated or created through modelling and can be modified through conditioning, through both positive and negative reinforcement. Post-radical behaviourists accept the mentalistic processes of rule-making but continue to support the idea that the study is of the behaviour, the utterances and the responses to utterances.

Summary

The behaviourist movement has a long history and has influenced many areas of education.

The major aspects of behaviourism are classical conditioning, operant conditioning, modelling and language acquisition. The stimulus, response and consequence model underpins the concepts of conditioning and behaviour modification that drives the pedagogic processes. These have resulted in a number of therapeutic as well as educational strategies.

The behaviourist principles arising directly from the work of B. F. Skinner and Albert Bandura are as follows:

■ behaviour that is positively reinforced will more readily reoccur (enabled by direct and indirect rewards);
■ intermittent reinforcement is particularly effective (enabled by scheduling);
■ learning experiences should be presented in small amounts (identified through task analysis),
■ so that the responses can be reinforced and complex objectives achieved (enabled by shaping);
■ reinforcements generalise across similar stimuli producing secondary conditioning;
■ learners model behaviour so the teacher should demonstrate self-efficacy; and

- self-efficacy should be fostered through the behaviour modification interventions.

The next chapter describes the application of the behaviourist theories in classroom practice.

Activities

- Consider, in the light of the content of the chapter, the different aspects of behaviourism and the way in which the theories may indicate the efficacy of particular teaching strategies.
- Consider the strategies relating to how we respond to pupils that you have used, or witnessed being used, in teaching.

4

Pedagogy

By the end of this chapter you will be able to:

- identify the theories of pedagogy relating to the behaviourist classroom;
- identify approaches that are designed to support learning in a behaviourist classroom;
- identify approaches to curriculum design; and
- identify the basis for planning teaching with regard to behaviourist theories.

In this chapter, we consider pedagogy with respect to behaviourism, that is, how teachers can operate within the epistemology and how they can apply the theories outlined in the previous chapter. We have seen that behaviourist teaching is based on the belief that learning occurs when the appropriate responses are reinforced and inappropriate responses are ignored or punished. Learning is an active process of building more and more complex responses as the reinforcement becomes more focused and the responses more refined under the varying and developing reinforcements. We have also seen how new behaviours are established through modelling. Behaviourist learning theory strongly underpins pedagogy and a wide range of teaching strategies. Those strategies enhance and enable the learning environment and the preparedness of the learner to learn.

The characteristics of a behaviourist pedagogy

Behaviourist teaching is associated with learning that is contextualised, kinaesthetic, practical, visual, verbal and motivated. It is learning that is structured, sequenced, didactic, efficient and effective. These aspects of learning will be considered further, and also reflected in the last chapter of this book in a selection of vignette-style case studies.

The behaviourist teacher is one who understands the importance of sequencing the learning activities identified by task analysis of the learning objectives. Through modelling, shaping and chaining together responses, they enable the learners to acquire complex and refined responses to a wide range of events and prompts. Progress is secured and learning takes place when the appropriate behaviours are positively reinforced, and so self-efficacy and the social and emotional aspects of learning are enhanced. Motivation, collectivism and social community are enhanced through token economies, positive classroom management and the modelling of appropriate behaviours by adults. The behaviourist teacher has strategies to support working in the new agendas of 'Every Child Matters', personalisation, assessment for learning, diversity and inclusion.

The chapter is divided into several discussions. The first describes the basic pedagogy arising from considering positive reinforcement. The second deals with how the curriculum and the focus of teaching is analysed and presented to ensure learning takes place and progress is established. The third section describes the different strategies that are employed to enhance the process of reinforcement, including rote learning, prompting, scheduling, contracts, the token economy and sanctuary. Finally, there is a consideration of the strategies for removing unwanted behaviours and a discussion of punishment.

Behaviour modification through positive reinforcement

Behavioural or operant conditioning occurs when a response to a stimulus is positively reinforced. It is important to recall the principles:

- the reinforcer must follow the response;
- the reinforcer must follow immediately; and
- the reinforcer must be contingent on the response.

Timing, magnitude and consistency of reinforcement can all influence the rate at which new behaviours are learned.

In the classroom this reinforcement can come from three areas: intrinsically from the learner's self-motivations, extrinsically as part of the mechanisms of teaching and extrinsically as a result of the direct and personalised actions of the teacher. All three are important aspects of the behaviourist pedagogy and they are illustrated in Figure 4.1. The more the association between the stimulus and response is rewarded the more sustained the conditioning and the more likely that the response will occur in the absence of the reward.

> This is the ambition of the strategies, that they establish patterns of behaviour and responses that become habitualised and so create situations where learning can become independent of the extrinsic reinforcement.

The intrinsic reinforcers are the more difficult to control yet are very powerful in the process of reinforcement. If the association between stimulus, say, the opportunity to quietly read, and the positively reinforced response of, say, quietly reading, is established by both the extrinsic reward of praise or approval and by the intrinsic response of satisfaction, then the satisfaction reinforcer can continue to motivate the learner long after the extrinsic reward has been removed.

> This is the ambition of the strategies, that they establish patterns of behaviour and responses that become reinforced through intrinsic reinforcement and so create situations where learning can become independent of the extrinsic reinforcement.

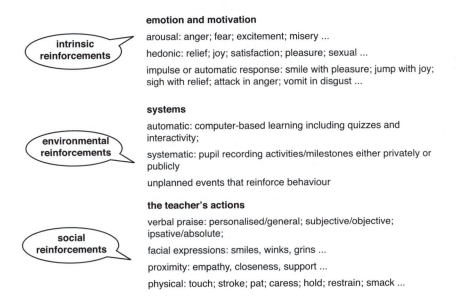

intrinsic reinforcements

emotion and motivation

arousal: anger; fear; excitement; misery ...

hedonic: relief; joy; satisfaction; pleasure; sexual ...

impulse or automatic response: smile with pleasure; jump with joy; sigh with relief; attack in anger; vomit in disgust ...

environmental reinforcements

systems

automatic: computer-based learning including quizzes and interactivity;

systematic: pupil recording activities/milestones either privately or publicly

unplanned events that reinforce behaviour

social reinforcements

the teacher's actions

verbal praise: personalised/general; subjective/objective; ipsative/absolute;

facial expressions: smiles, winks, grins ...

proximity: empathy, closeness, support ...

physical: touch; stroke; pat; caress; hold; restrain; smack ...

Figure 4.1 Classroom conditioning through reinforcement

The impulse responses that learners make are very useful signs for the teacher to determine whether a particular stimulus is likely to evoke a response appropriate for establishing and sustaining learning. An angry or fearful response is not a positive reinforcer, and the stimulus is unlikely to reinforce learning.

The environmental reinforcements are the classroom systems that are in place which systematically reinforce. Systematic reinforcement can be established through the teaching resources that are in place. In all teaching, it is important to identify and communicate clearly defined outcomes. The learning outcomes or behavioural objectives should be sequenced and reflect the results of a task analysis of the curriculum. In the next section we will see how the task analysis of a curriculum and its presentation as a sequence of objectives both facilitates and is enhanced by positive reinforcement.

Creating a curriculum

In most settings the overall aims and content of the curriculum are made explicit. These may take the form of examination specifications, programmes of study, levels of attainment, criteria of assessment or simply a textbook specifying experience and activity. Whatever the situation, the teacher takes responsibility for presenting that curriculum in the form of lesson-by-lesson events, supplementary work (homework) and alternative activities, for example, online resources. Each lesson event is planned and usually segmented to provide stimulus and experience intermixed with opportunities for practice and reinforcement. Task analysis provides the mechanism for the teacher to divide the curriculum into achievable, measurable and hence reinforceable activities.

The curriculum may consist of:

- *skills development* – for example, the cognitive process of analysing a word-based mathematical problem and converting to a numeric process, or a psychomotor activity like copying and pasting information from a web page to a word-processed document, or the physical task of using a burette to measure liquid required to reach the turning point of an indicator;
- *knowledge acquisition* – for example, learning facts and figures to support other cognitive processes, or visual recognition of signs and symbols, or knowing the correct procedures in particular situations;
- *demonstration or application of learning (reflecting understanding)* – for example, creating a computer program to solve a problem or simulate a situation; or
- *development of attitudes or opinions* – for example, in circle time, hot seating or debating scenarios.

This is a traditional way of thinking about teaching. The outcomes are divided into skills, knowledge, understanding and attitudes (SKUA). The learning activities and opportunities are created to develop all four areas. The more challenging and interesting aspects of teaching are developing the students' understanding of concepts and the development of their affective domain (Bloom, 1956). These two areas are also more challenging when considering assessment.

The SKUA analysis is adapted from the seminal work *Curriculum 11–16: Towards a Statement of Entitlement: Curriculum Reappraisal in Action* (DES, 1983).

- *skills* – repeat as an observable performance;
- *knowledge* – recall of factual truths;
- *understanding* – explain (verbal behaviour) in other contexts; and
- *attitudes* – describe in terms of self and others.

This analysis of the curriculum has since been developed and presented as:

- know that … (knowledge: factual information, for example, names, places, symbols, formulae, events);
- develop/be able to … (skills: using knowledge, applying techniques, analysing information, etc.);
- understand how/why … (understanding: concepts, reasons, effects, principles, processes, etc.); and
- develop/be aware of … (attitudes and values: empathy, caring, sensitivity towards social issues, feelings, moral issues, etc.)

in the Key Stage 3 training materials (advisory materials for England and Wales) for the foundation subjects (DfES, 2002).

Bloom's Taxonomy (Bloom, 1956) offers an insight into these analyses of curriculum to aid the process of task analysis. It supports the classification of objectives that, in turn, helps with the selection of instructional methods, media of teaching, materials and resources to be used and the assessment and evaluation procedures that are appropriate. There are three primary domains: cognitive, psychomotor and affective.

The action words of the cognitive domain are:

- *knowledge*: arrange, define, duplicate, label, list, find, memorise, name, order, search, remember, recognise, relate, recall, repeat, identify, locate;
- *comprehension*: classify, describe, discuss, indicate, locate, recognise, report, restate, review, select, translate, interpret, explain, express, identify;
- *application*: apply, choose, demonstrate, dramatise, employ, illustrate, interpret, operate, practise, schedule, sketch, solve, use, write, utilise, exemplify;

- *analysis*: analyse, appraise, calculate, categorise, compare, contrast, criticise, differentiate, discriminate, distinguish, examine, experiment, question, test;
- *synthesis*: arrange, assemble, sequence, build, collect, design, develop, formulate, manage, organise, plan, prepare, compose, construct, create, propose, set up, produce, program, write;
- *evaluation*: appraise, score, choose, compare, defend, judge, predict, rate, select, support, value, argue, cost, assess, attach, grade, evaluate.

An important step in task analysis is identifying learning outcomes expressed as behavioural objectives and frequently called instructional objectives, targets, functional objectives or behavioural objectives or learning outcomes. Because the cognitive domain's six levels of operation are described in 'doing' words, they can be specified as behavioural objectives. It should be noted that Lorin Anderson, a former student of Benjamin Bloom, revised the cognitive domain in the learning taxonomy and made important changes to the naming of the six categories from nouns to verbs. Again, this emphasised the behavioural aspects of the domain. The new terms drawn from the work of Anderson and Krathwohl are exemplified as:

- *remembering*: retrieving, recognising, and recalling relevant knowledge from long-term memory and includes listing, reciting and defining;
- *understanding*: constructing meaning from oral, written, and graphic messages through interpreting, exemplifying, classifying, summarising, inferring, comparing, and explaining;
- *applying*: carrying out or using a procedure through executing, or implementing and using the procedures in novel situations;
- *analysing*: breaking material into constituent parts, determining how the parts relate to one another and to an overall structure or purpose through differentiating, organising, and attributing including the representation of ideas through diagrams, charts, models and graphics;
- *evaluating*: making judgments based on criteria and standards through checking and critiquing with associated actions of judging, assessing, rating, selecting, choosing, comparing, arguing, criticising, deducing, validating, inferring and concluding;
- *creating*: putting elements together to form a coherent or functional whole; reorganising elements into a new pattern or structure through generating, planning, or producing with associated actions of composing (graphical, aural or visual forms), inventing/originating (novel applications), modifying, formulating, generalising and predicting. (Based on Anderson and Krathwohl, 2001: 67–8)

It is important to differentiate the fundamental difference between types of objectives and the concept of aims. Imagine being an archer. The aim is the act of drawing back the bow and directing the arrow. The aim is the intention; your aim is to hit the target. The target is the objective. The target is at a set distance and a set size. The target is specified as a set of rings and the value placed upon each ring. Objectives are specific, outcome-based and measurable. The acronym SMART is often used with various words associated with the letters:

- **S**pecific
- **M**easurable
- **A**chievable
- **R**einforceable
- **T**imely

Objectives are the foundation upon which learning sequences can be built, and they are also the foundation for assessments that inform both the learner and the teacher of progress and attainment. The objectives need not limit the learning activities or the exploration of the topic but they do ensure that the learning is focused. The objectives are specific; they are outcome-based and state what the learner should be able to do after the learning is complete. The way in which the learning happens is not considered in an objective; that is for the teacher and the learner to decide. However, the specification of the objectives is part of the teachers' responsibilities and requires their professional understanding. A basic guide to the important considerations is ABCD: A is considering the audience; B is the overt/measurable behaviour the learners are to carry out; C is the conditions of where and when; and D is the degree or measure of the level of attainment.

The objectives are measurable; they should describe learning outcomes that can be observed or recorded in some tangible way. The evidence that learning has taken place is often important, and the current trend to adopt electronic portfolios and provide evidence for specific criteria reinforces the teachers' activity of specifying the sorts of evidence that the learning outcomes will provide. The behaviourist teacher might reflect that 'I cannot see the learner understanding, but I can see them applying their understanding'.

The objectives are achievable. In the next section there is discussion of situations when positive reinforcement can become ineffectual, and one area is when the expected or required step is too great. The art of task analysis is the balance between making the tasks large enough to be interesting and valuable but not so large that the individual cannot achieve them. The equivalent consideration is that the tasks have to be small enough for the learners to achieve but not trivial and therefore valueless for reinforcement, or so atomistic of the curriculum that the big ideas and concepts are lost. Achievable objectives lead to success.

The objectives are reinforceable; they should be designed so that any required behaviour modification techniques can be put in place.

Objectives should be timely; they should be timely in terms of frequency, duration and occurrence. Objectives that are too frequent may tire the learner whereas too infrequent may bore the learner. Objectives given too short a duration may cause unnecessary failure – failure because of the lack of time rather than failing to be able to carry out the task. Objectives given too long a duration make for inefficient teaching and delayed progress through the scheme of work. The timing of the occurrence of the objective is important. Placing targets at inappropriate times of the day or parts of the programme can affect attainment.

The connecting of independent SMART outcomes to form a sequence should consider these progressions:

- from simple to complex;
- from known to unknown;
- from the particular to the general; and
- from the physical to the verbal.

Milestones are those points between each activity of the sequence. It is at the milestones that the positive reinforcement can be systematically established. Those reinforcers focus upon recognition and celebration of the completion of the task. It is the nature of the class that determines whether reinforcement should be covert (confidential to the learner and the teacher) or overt (with the whole class being aware). Covert systems include the child marking it on their personal record of progress or informing the teacher to mark it on the teacher's record of progress (mark book). That process may include the extrinsic reinforcement of praise from the teacher. Again, the degree of involvement of the teacher will reflect the reinforcement needs of the individual and of the class as a whole. Overt recognition of progress through the milestones includes the learner marking an open-access chart of everyone's results or informing the teacher, who can give class-wide praise to the individual.

The role of overt praise and the celebration of success through charts, displays and record books are important for the positive reinforcement of the individual learner. The learner is also demonstrating behaviour that others may model and therefore promotes similar behaviours – positively receiving praise as a result of achieving success and making progress in classroom activities.

One particular application of this form of curriculum analysis and

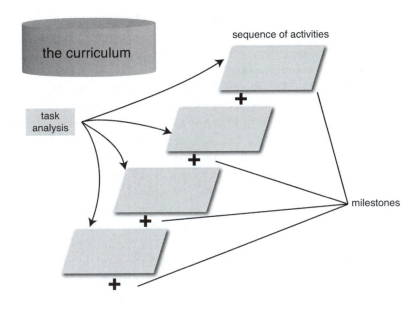

Figure 4.2 Task analysis of the curriculum creating activities and milestones

presentation of work is programmed learning, or programmed instruction. This description is taken from *Walden Two*:

> In this device [teaching machine], a human learner is given a logically connected series of questions or problems, to each of which there is one correct answer from among the alternative answers offered by the machine. If the learner selects a wrong answer, the machine provides an explanation of the error and directs the student back to a clarifying point in the sequence. If the learner selects the right answer, the machine tells him that he is right and sends him on to the next question. (Skinner, 1948: 6–7)

Although programmed learning machines are no longer used, there are emulated in the structures of some computer-based applications such as integrated learning systems (ILS), open integrated learning systems (OILS) and standards when constructing learning objects, for example, SCORM compliancy. SCORM (Shareable Content Object Reference Model) is a standard for developing and delivering teaching materials for online training courses and virtual learning environments (VLE). The compliancy standards ensure that developers could find, import, share, reuse and export learning materials. It is necessary to be very specific about the construction, sequencing and assessment of learning objects. ILSs are networked computers providing instructional content as well as assessment and management tools. Instruction is organised around specific objectives, and the software is based on a mastery learning approach to instruction. A current example is SuccessMaker (Pearson, 2009). The principles are based on the implications of reinforcement theory (Markle, 1969; Skinner, 1968) and require the curriculum to be presented as a series of frames.

Mastery learning is based on the premise that all children can learn when the appropriate conditions are provided; it has its origins in the work of Bloom (1968, 1974). Bloom was trying to improve the effectiveness of traditional classroom instruction and identified that assessment was an important element. The common habit of teaching a module of work and assessing at the end was not particularly effective. He therefore promoted a two-part assessment based on criterion, diagnostic and formative principles. In a mastery learning module, all the learners are introduced to the topic and the learning activities. Each activity is assessed formatively, that is, each is assessed in such a way that the teacher and the learner are informed of the areas of error and areas of success. Successful learners proceed through the module that is supplemented with enrichment activities, whilst those not succeeding are given further support, correction of their mistakes and re-assessment. In mastery learning, learners do not move to new learning objectives until they develop proficiency in the current objectives. This form of teaching requires accurate task analysis to ensure that the steps are logical and sequential. It affords personalised learning, cooperation and collaboration between peers, high success rates (Kulik, Kulik and Bangert-Downs, 1990) and clear measures of progress. Subsequently, other approaches were devised, including Personalised System for Instruction (PSI), Problem-Based Learning (PBL), Assessment for Learning (AFL) and Outcome-Based Education (OBE). In all cases, the pattern of instruction is divided into units with assessments supporting learning and progress being measured by the number of units successfully completed. In Skinner's approach the smallest elements of teaching are called frames.

Frames take the form of a stimulus (question) and response (answer). They:

- are sequential;.
- expose the learner to the subject in gradual steps;
- require that the learner make a response for every frame;
- provide immediate feedback;
- present the questions so the response is usually correct;
- present positive reinforcement.

The teacher or other learners can supplement the environmental positive reinforcement with social reinforcement; that can be in the form of verbal praise, prizes, tokens or good marks. The main source of automated response is the computer-based teaching applications. They range from the narrowly focused quizzes with right or wrong answers through to open searching of a high quantity of data to seek patterns, commonality or conclusions. Some systems also include opportunities for social interaction with the associated modelling of behaviour. These aspects of classroom psychology will be dealt with fully in the companion book on theories and practice, *Psychology for the Classroom: E-learning*.

We turn now to that part of the curriculum that may not be planned for with the same degree of rigour. The classroom environment is complex and dynamic and events happen that are unexpected – if that is good then it is serendipity. Other things occur purposefully but without overt declaration – that is the hidden curriculum. Serendipity occurs when those events offer positive reinforcement of appropriate behaviours. One cannot plan for the head teacher to arrive with visitors the very moment the class falls into a quiet period of constructive work. The relief and gratitude of the head teacher is clearly apparent, perhaps overtly expressed in praise to the pupils and certainly they are praised immediately after the event. The craft of teaching is to maximise the probability of those unexpected opportunities for positive reinforcement and also to ensure that, when they occur, they do not go unnoticed. The classroom that is fully immersed in the strategies of the social and emotional aspects of learning (Weare and Gray, 2003) will be rich in positive reinforcement of the individual's appropriate behaviour from the responses of the other pupils and the response of the teacher and other adults.

The term 'hidden curriculum' was reportedly coined by Philip Jackson in his book *Life in Classrooms* (Jackson, 1968) and focused on the socialisation aspects of education. The term has been used in other contexts but the underlying meaning can be described as a process that is taking place where learners change their behaviour, not as a result of explicit aims and objectives, but as a result of covert, intentional aims or unintentional by-products of their experience. The unintentional aims can be a result of the modelling fully described in Chapters 2 and 3, whereby behaviour is initiated and modified through the social contact and observation of others. This may have both positive and negative effects as Bandura's Bobo the Clown investigations revealed. It is the responsibility of teachers to recognise the power of such modelling and to suppress the inappropriate behaviours of some learners, not just for their own sake, but also for the sakes of other learners.

The intentional but covert aims of the teacher to modify behaviour and enhance learning can take several forms, illustrated by these simple examples:

- The teacher structures a lesson considering taste in popular music with overt aims and reinforced objectives relating to listening in silence to a piece of music and making just two positive comments afterwards. The covert aim is to condition the behaviours so that new experiences are more readily accepted by the learners and that they have a strategy for describing them avoiding rejection and negativity.

■ On a school visit the teacher designs the activity sheet to require pupils to identify simple facts and figures from the displays and environment with rewards associated with completeness of the activity. The covert aim is to expose the learners to a new experience, historical or geographical or social, to develop their interest in other activities.

■ At the school disco the explicit rules and positive reinforcers are associated with following the conventions of standing, talking, drinking, asking for a dance, accepting invitations, dancing and returning to friends. The covert intention is for the learners to acquire social skills and interests.

The hidden curriculum is an important aspect of our learners' education. It is so important that we must foster this naturalistic exposure as well as making the explicit reference in terms of objectives.

Enhancing the interventions

The basic principles of behaviourism are the reinforcement of behaviour and the modelling of new behaviours. The ways in which teachers deploy the techniques of behaviourism reflect the needs of the learners, the context of learning and the curriculum. There are many established ways in which those principles can be implemented and those interventions can be enhanced.

Rote learning

Hermann Ebbinghaus (1885) conducted a wide range of experiments focused upon simple rote; they have stood the test of time and contribute much of what is known about rote learning and retention today. His research drew a number of conclusions (as outlined in Chapter 2). The pedagogic implications relate to five aspects of teaching rote learning strategies:

1 Better results are achieved by distributing the learning trials over a longer period of time, which is more effective than concentrating practice into a shorter period. For example, the rote learning of a spelling list or the elements of the halogen family is better achieved by practice once a week rather than seven times in a single lesson, which is better than seven times in the course of 2 minutes.

2 The items that occur near the start and near the end of the list are more readily

remembered (primacy and recency). Where there are more important items, they should be placed at the start or the end. The rehearsal for a shopping visit could be coffee, sugar, bubble bath, biscuits and milk or, in the case of organising an experiment, scales, chemicals, notepaper, ruler and help sheet.

3 Preparation for learning is important and even small amounts of prior learning makes relearning more effective: 'Tomorrow we are going to be studying the halogen family, and so for homework tonight, write out the names of the halogens and their symbols'.

4 It is important to continue to practise the activity after the learning criterion has been reached. For example, there are some words that are frequently misspelt by trainee teachers: *separate, definite, definitely, appropriate, practice* and *practise* (a grammar issue), *rehearsal,* etc. After the initial rote learning activity, periodic attention is drawn to the words. The revision activity enhances retention.

5 In later experiments Ebbinghaus showed that replacing nonsense words with meaningful words increased the ease of learning and the rates of retention – the implication is that it is not simply the mechanism of rote that teachers should be concerned with but also that of meaning and other aspects such as visualisation, context and social impact.

Ebbinghaus made another important discovery called savings. Savings refers to the amount of information retained in the subconscious even after this information had been completely forgotten. It is information that cannot be consciously accessed. One might think that such mentalistic considerations are outside the domain of behaviourists, but in this case, savings simply explains an observed and repeatable behaviour pattern. To test the phenomenon, Ebbinghaus memorised a list of items until he could recall them perfectly. He would then not access the list until he could not recall any of the list. When he relearned the list, the new learning curve showed that the second list was generally memorised faster. The difference between the two learning curves is what Ebbinghaus called savings. The implication for pedagogy is that we should attempt to arrange different aspects of knowledge on similar structures to lower the overheads of learning. Also, we should foster a greater value in our learners' learning at a younger age and the fact that it has lasting value long after it has apparently been forgotten.

Prompting

The majority of strategies employed to change or eliminate current behaviours or introduce new behaviours are based upon contingency reinforcements

– when something happens a response is managed to either positively reinforce the behaviour or to reduce the probability or severity of the behaviour. There are a number of strategies, called stimulus control, that operate on the antecedents of behaviours with a major one being modelling and another being the provision of information. Prompting is a stimulus control strategy. The value of antecedent strategies is that they can introduce new behaviours. The reinforcement strategies can only enhance or promote behaviours that are already taking place.

Prompts are signals that indicate what actions are appropriate.

'I am a teacher trainer. I meet my trainees on many occasions in university teaching sessions, during social occasions, in the library and on the Internet. We never make physical contact. When I walk into their classroom, in front of their pupils I will put forward my hand and it will prompt the handshake – a behaviour that has never occurred between us before that. The prompt indicates the appropriate behaviour'.

Prompts can take many forms, from the direct ('Do not talk' sign) to the subtle, the verbal ('Check you have everything'), the visual (a textbook reminder to make a note!), the auditory (teacher ringing a bell for attention), the kinaesthetic (cell phone on vibrate) or the physical (teacher pointing at the book). It is the directness and timeliness of prompts that give them potency to change and initiate behaviours. The following passage clearly describes the behaviourist view regarding the effectiveness of information and the effectiveness of prompts.

The mere presentation of information through instructions, slogans, pamphlets or articles is typically ineffective, even though huge amounts of money and paper are spent on such endeavours. Although common sense suggests that we need to educate people about environmental problems, education in itself does very little to change behaviour. Such an outcome is not surprising to behaviourists, who have argued all along that attitudes and awareness do not necessarily indicate much about actions. To a behaviourist, attitudes are forms of verbal behaviour that may or may not be correlated with other behaviours. Thus, there is no reason to believe that education alone would change what people actually do, a view supported by many studies (Du Nann Winter and Koger, 2004: 98; Du Nann Winter cites Gardner and Stern (2002) for supporting evidence).

Prompting is a powerful strategy in the behaviourist teacher's classroom in changing and initiating appropriate behaviours before the behaviour occurs.

Scheduling

Behaviours, whether physical activities or expressed attitudes, are modi-fied through positive reinforcement. The way in which that reinforcement is managed is called scheduling. Differential reinforcements are patterns of positive reinforcement that are not always and consistently applied at a one-to-one level with the response. They are usually applied systematically or conditionally. Skinner discovered that conditioning could be optimised through a pattern of repeated and reduced positive reinforcement of the desired behaviours. He established that schedules of reinforcement are important components of the learning process and impact on the strength, rate, extinction and re-establishment of the responses. Bandura observed that children repeatedly seeking attention from parents tend to be those randomly reinforced by their parents (Bandura and Walters, 1963).

Two types of reinforcement schedules are continuous reinforcement and partial (intermittent) reinforcement, with four schedules of partial reinforce-ment: fixed-ratio, variable-ratio, fixed-interval and variable-interval schedules. (These are described in more detail in Chapter 3.) In summary, continuous reinforcement is important for the initial stages of learning; initial learning requires more reinforcement than later learning; rapid learning is associated with rapid extinction; and random ratio reinforcement has the slowest rate of extinction, that is, the information is remembered better. The pedagogic implications relate to planning a new curriculum and changing the classroom situation.

In planning a new curriculum the first stage is the task analysis and iden-tification of a sequence of learning activities with the interspaced milestones (see Creating a curriculum, p. 66). All change benefits from a period of continuous reinforcement. However, introducing a new curriculum, whether at the level of topic, theme, module, unit, course or examination programme, may actually be a previous occurrence and reinforced experience. Appropriate responses may already be established, and it is not necessary to have continu-ous reinforcement but rely on the partial reinforcement of a variable ratio. A structured curriculum of learning objectives and positively reinforced milestones is, in fact, a schedule of fixed-ratio reinforcement.

The second situation is making a change to the current pattern of working, usually remediating a situation where learning is not taking place. Examples are dealing with a disruptive class; working with disruptive individuals; or accommodating a small group of disruptive learners. Here, the environ-ment is likely to be chaotic at some level, and there are not clear patterns of expected behaviours, there are not clear reinforcers and the systems are certainly not in place to accommodate new activities and attitude changes.

The reinforcement must start with a continuous schedule until stability is established. The starting point for the teacher is task analysis and establishing as a sequence of objectives that build to create a learning environment. They have been identified as getting the attention of the learners; being prepared for learning; working with transitions; and working with grades. The full scenario is described in the final vignette of the next chapter. Each new objective has to be introduced with continuous reinforcement but the nature of the objective will determine which form of schedule is most appropriate. Examples are gaining the attention of the learners, fixed ratio; learners' preparedness, variable ratio; coping with transitions, variable interval; and handling grades, random ratio.

Contingency contracts

Contracts and agreements are part of the pedagogy of behaviourism. They enhance and focus the processes of reinforcement and behaviour modification. A behaviour contract is an agreement between the learner and teacher about how the individual will behave. It indicates the consequence should the learner not behave according to the contract and it also states the reinforcer that is used for successful compliance or completion. The form of the contract can range from an informal verbal agreement through to a written statement signed off by the teacher and learner or learners. There are two parts to all contracts: the activity or attitude (as expressed through physical or verbal behaviour) and the reinforcer (reward) that the learner or learners receive upon completion. The detail must eliminate the possibility of dispute at a later stage if the teacher and learner disagree whether the contract has been fulfilled. The use of SMART behavioural objects is therefore important.

The selection of the reinforcers is also important. They have to be reinforcing and, because the writing of the contract involves negotiation, there may also need to be compromise between what the learner wants and what the teacher thinks they should receive. Reinforcers that support learners' learning can become self-fulfilling. If a learning activity − say, completing some puzzles − is positively reinforced by another learning activity − say, being given free-reading time − the process of learning becomes reinforced. When negotiating reinforcers the teacher should provide a range of reinforcers. The learner being enabled to make a choice is also being supported in their self-efficacy.

Learning contracts include: the goal (learning outcome or appropriate behaviour); the methods or monitoring and recording; the method and conditions of reward; the consequences of not completing; and the time limits and process of review. The behaviour contract provides the learner with structure and the opportunity for self-management, again leading to self-efficacy, and is therefore an effective form of behaviour modification.

It is important to differentiate between the strategic planning of a contract as an intervention to change the long-term behaviour and attitude of a learner and the use of lures. 'A lure is a reward offered just before a behaviour in order to get it to occur. It differs from a contract in that, while both specify contingencies, a contract is established well before a problem or opportunity to respond occurs' (Vargas, 2009: 178). Lures are an antecedent reward. It is a reward that occurs before the behaviour and is not part of the behaviour modification tranche of strategies. It is explained by Vargas: 'If Skinner wanted the dog to jump, he could have tied a piece of tempting meat high on the wall where the dog would have to jump to reach it' (2009: 178) but take away the meat and the dog does not jump. The behaviourist approach is to say 'jump' and if the dog jumps they get a morsel of meat. After a little more reinforcement the dog will jump on command and only intermittent reinforcers will be needed to sustain the behaviour. The behaviourist teacher does not say, 'Do your work well and I will give you a sweet'. The lure does not create sustained behaviour.

The token economy is often associated with contracts between the teacher and learner whereby particular positive acts are rewarded by a token. The token economy is an effective approach that impacts upon individuals and whole communities. It can be used to simultaneously reinforce a wide range of activities and attitudes with a number of individuals or with the community as a whole. It is therefore an aid to drawing up contracts and identifying appropriate reinforcers. The token economy is the focus of a vignette in the final chapter.

Shaping

Shaping is a technique of establishing a complex behaviour through stages. It occurs by first reinforcing a behaviour that is similar to the desired behaviour. Further reinforcement is provided as closer behaviours are exhibited. Eventually, only the desired behaviour is reinforced.

Consider learning to ride a bicycle. Most of us learn through some extrinsic reinforcement of success provided by a parent but all of us learn through the extrinsic reinforcement provided by the bicycle staying in an upright position with us safely perched on the saddle. Inappropriate behaviours such as turning the handlebars too sharply or putting the brakes on too quickly are sadly punished. When we first get on the bicycle, regardless of all the modelling experienced and all of the knowledge given, we begin as novices, and it is through the process of shaping we achieve the status of competent and confident cyclists. At the start, we are positively reinforced because our irregular but purposeful swings of the handlebars keep us in the upright position. We learn to control the wobble and the bicycle ceases to give the reinforcement. Our next challenge is turning. Again, we experiment with the handlebars and balance of our body and on successful turning the bicycle remains upright and we are not punished. We perfect the turning process and look for new challenges, say riding with one hand. This whole process is one of shaping with the positive reinforcement changing from one behaviour to the next as the behaviours move towards the final goal of competent and confident riding.

Some behaviourists describe shaping as an evolutionary process akin to the Darwinian concept of the evolution of species (Baum, 2005). Evolution does not have a specified endpoint but is a process of continual change in response to the environment. In a similar way, the learner continually develops their skills (and some skills become extinct) because of the reinforcement effects taking place. 'Just as differences in reproductive success (fitness) shape the composition of a population of genotypes, so reinforcement and punishment shape the composition of an individual's behaviour' (Baum, 2005: 78). Both assume a gradual change through time.

Tokens and the token economy

The behaviourist theory is based upon positive reinforcement or reward to change behaviour or increase the frequency or probability of an appropriate behaviour. The necessity for rewarding is the basis of the token economy in which appropriate behaviour is positively reinforced by a token to represent the back-up reinforcer. It is not always feasible or appropriate to be giving rewards of an immediate value in the learning setting. By giving tokens that represent awards, the same sorts of behaviour modification can be achieved as by the use of real rewards. Within the classroom, school or any learning environment the token economy can help the teacher reward. It is a significant step towards self-efficacy because the learner is accepting some form of deferment of reward. They are having more opportunity to reflect upon their behaviour and, hopefully, adopt the behaviour without future reward.

The back-up reinforcers are the meaningful objects, privileges or activities that individuals receive in exchange for their tokens. The rewards can be social (praise and approval), tangible (sweets, toys or items of value) or virtual (privilege, status or entry to lotteries giving access to a higher probability of receiving an enhanced reward). Individuals are motivated to earn tokens in anticipation of the future reward represented by the tokens, and so the success of a token economy depends upon the appeal of the back-up reinforcers.

The token economy can be highly sophisticated and institutionalised or very simple and informal. For example, it can be a simple penny-in-the-jar – the learner is given a penny to place in a jar. There is the promise of a reward when the jar is full, or there are ten coins, or the learner decides to trade them. As an incentive, the value at trade-in can be more than the sum of the pennies – perhaps a visit to a shopping arcade. This is an example of a simple deferment technique with the tangible value of the back-up reinforcer being high.

The rules of rewarding behaviour or achievement with tokens are the same as the general rules for positive reinforcement. The rewards should be timely and immediate (following the appropriate response), affective (having an impact), consistent and contingent upon the behaviour. Tokens offer flexibility over the traditional immediate reinforcers. The rewarding process is less likely to get in the way of the desired behaviour. For example, rewarding a student's on-task behaviour with an off-task activity defeats the purpose of the reinforcement, but rewarding on-task behaviour with a token that represents the promise of the same off-task activity does not interfere with the continuing on-task behaviour. The same tokens can be used for several interventions simultaneously or sequentially. Here are two examples. The first is a primary school pupil who has four different target areas for development: being on-task (being rewarded intermittently during lesson times with a single token to a covert maximum of five per teaching session), playing sociably in the playground (two tokens awarded every playtime when no incident of his unsociable behaviour is noted), eating his packed lunch completely (five tokens) and arriving at school (a token is given when he is seated with his coat off and reader in front of him). The second example is the token economy operating in a class of secondary school girls reluctantly following an examination course. During each module, the reward contract is changed to reflect the differing outputs required, ranging from possessing the skills to draw a line graph on the computer to completing a 1,000-word report on a local residential development. In both examples, the token is flexible and is less probable that the learners will reach a point of satiation. Tokens have flexibility because any member of staff can give the reward. In some token economies, other learners are empowered to reward with tokens. The reward can be automatic and even built into virtual learning environments on completion of on-screen tasks.

The rewards of a token can be formally presented or informally or covertly awarded. The learner may be slipped a merit card for them to hand to another teacher for recognition or accumulation. In the busy classroom it is easier for the tokens to be readily available for award and easily given. It could be a rubber stamp and inkpad, a set of preprinted cards, a sheet of stickers or simply the teacher drawing a smiley face in the book. In the ICT room, it can be the teacher adding the token on-screen to the shared document that all pupils can read but to which only the teacher can write.

The rewards can be associated with a group or an individual. For example, on completion of a group task, rewards can be associated with the quality of the work, and each contributor receives the same number of tokens. A more sophisticated system associated with a group project awards a number of tokens as a reward for the quality of the project – however, the learners have to divide the tokens between each other on the basis of who they feel deserves the award based upon their contribution to the overall project. This is an example of the hidden curriculum in practice. The explicit aims of the project work relate to collaboration and cooperation – the token sharing activity is not explicitly targeted with reinforcements but has an important impact upon the exercise of the collaboration skills.

The system can apply to the whole school whereby, at the point of reward, the teacher formally or informally issues a token; the learner takes respons-ibility for the accumulation or passes it to another teacher for recording and celebration and eventually they are tallied for individual, group or whole school celebration and reward. A vignette in the next chapter illustrates how this system is effectively used in a conventional secondary school. In all token economies there needs to be a system for exchanging tokens which usually means trading in for an expected reward or purchasing from a choice of back-up reinforcers. The token value of each back-up reinforcer can be predetermined based on monetary value, demand or educational value. For example, if the reinforcer is expensive or highly attractive, the token value should be higher. As part of the reinforcement process, if the reinforcer would support the learning process, the token value of it should be lower. The judgement about the value of the back-up reinforcers is as crucial as deciding what activities are to be reinforced by the tokens. If rewards are too costly in terms of the number of tokens required to receive the reward then the learners are disincentified.

Where a token economy is school-wide there need to be steps taken to ensure consistent implementation by teachers. In order for the token eco-nomy to succeed it must be seen to be fair. Learners who work consistently but not inspiringly must not be disenfranchised. Learners doing outstanding work are easily identified and rewarded. Learners struggling and making small progressions can also be rewarded. It is those middle-of-the-road learners who may be ignored. In an efficient token economy, good record-keeping is required and patterns of reward identified. Other problems associated with token economies include: inflation, counterfeiting, theft and exploitation. Inflation is associated with teachers' actions. It occurs when too many tokens are issued and their relative value is reduced when trading in for the back-up reinforcer, or they are too frequently awarded in the classroom and lose their impact. Learners may be responsible for counterfeiting and theft but there are strategies that can be adopted to reduce the probability or lessen the impact. In systems where the token is a card awarded by the teacher, they can be named. In systems where there are high numbers then poker-style chips can be used. The former reduces the tendency of theft and the second tackles counterfeiting. Exploitation occurs when the learner manipulates the teacher into awarding tokens and is a complex social situation that the experienced teacher can learn to avoid.

For some pupils the personalised approach is essential to establish the flexibility required to meet his or her changing needs. With imagination, the teacher can integrate the personal approach into the school system, but in many cases the systems operate independently. For example, the individual learner may receive tokens at the rate of 10 or 20 per lesson whereas the average pupil in the school receives five tokens per week. Using the same tokens would undermine the school system. The learner is issued with their tokens that lead to their reward but with an exchange rate so that they can also participate fairly in the school system. Where an individualised system is in place the recording of rewards and behaviour is essential. Before a programme begins, a baseline should be established so that the reward rate can be set at a suitable level or expectation. Changes in behaviour and the rate of reward are then recorded and this information is used to measure the individual's progress, as well as the effectiveness of the token economy.

The token economy is often associated with contracts or agreements between the teacher and learner whereby particular positive acts are rewarded by a token. Those positive acts can be the learner doing, being, appearing or completing in a predetermined way. Within a contract, the tokens are awarded more frequently and in higher amounts near the start, but as the learners respond, the opportunities to earn tokens become more demanding. Fading is the act of steadily decreasing the availability of tokens or the number of tokens awarded for an activity. By gradually decreasing the reinforcement by tokens, learners should independently carry out the desired behaviour. The use of social reinforcers aids the fading of token dependency and encourages a more naturalistic approach to conditioning whereby the reinforcer becomes internalised. The learner learns because of the intrinsic pleasure of learning.

The advantages of token economies are that behaviours can be rewarded immediately. It enables deferment of reward and learners having some control of the reward process. It encourages self-efficacy and brings learners a step closer to not requiring rewards. Under token economies the rewards can be the same for all members of a group; collaboration and team effort can be encouraged. The disadvantages include the cost-overheads associated with planning the structure, teacher time in implementing the scheme, staff training and the provision of tangible rewards. The token economy is a popular approach in many schools and that stands as testimony to its effectiveness and cost-efficiency.

SEAL, sanctuary and self-efficacy

The place of work should be a secure, rewarding and self-effectuating environment in which satisfaction and productivity go hand-in-hand – a right for all teachers. We should offer nothing less for our learners. Skinner described a utopia where social well-being was established through positive reinforcement by the authority upon the community in *Walden Two* (1948). The community was happy, productive and creative. In a similar way, the pedagogy arising from the consideration of positive reinforcement in a social classroom is built upon social, curriculum and behaviour considerations. Teachers should:

- identify a code of conduct or classroom rules regarding talking and learners' behaviour in general;
- make clear the learning objectives and outcomes through a systematic and consistent approach, for example, describing in learner-speak what the learners are learning to do and what the teacher is looking for and making clear the rationale for the subject content;
- identify the group-work skills, knowledge, understanding and attitudes that the learners need to develop to enable them to contribute as fully as possible;
- identify the affordances and challenges of competitive working within each context they teach;
- support the social and emotional development of learners through the whole-class and group-work discussions; and
- encourage cooperation and collaboration through action, instructions and advice.

The behaviourist teacher must be aware of the values and affordances of the behaviour strategies associated with positive reinforcement, contracts, task analysis and the token economy. One aspect of the behaviourist approach is to provide a sanctuary. There is a vignette in the next chapter describing the implementation of a sanctuary. The important principles are that the learner decides when to go; it is not a 'sin-bin' or a cooler where learners are sent as a punishment. The sanctuary promotes self-efficacy.

Learners' well-being is determined to a large extent by their feelings of self-efficacy brought about through a sense that they are in control of their environment and what will happen to them. During the 1960s, Bandura conducted a programme of research focusing on learners' self-regulatory capabilities. It played an important role in developing the behaviourist perspective from one where people were seen to be simply reacting to stimuli to one where they were impacting upon the environment and also acting in a self-regulatory way. In an interesting extension of the social learning experiments with Bobo the Clown, Bandura showed that children will emulate the adult model when it came to self-reward for performance. Similarly, learners seeing adults forego small immediate rewards in preference for larger deferred rewards had a tendency to behave similarly (Zimmerman and Schunk 2002: 8).

The pedagogy arising from these observations should be:

■ teacher-focused, whereby the teacher is a model of appropriate behaviour;
■ celebratory of learner success in the social as well as academic aspects of learning;
■ avoidant of any negative experiences (seeing inappropriate behaviours);
■ inclusive of self-rewarding, foregoing instant gratification for deferred reward: 'That was good lesson … I enjoyed teaching it … I deserve a reward … I will have some chocolates when I get home'.

Bandura also identified aspects of self-efficacy that are established through learners taking control of their behaviour. There are three aspects:

1 *self-observation* – the learner considers their behaviour and monitors it;
2 *judgement* – the learner compares themselves against a standard; and
3 *self-response* – the learner rewards themselves.

The pedagogy arising from these principles includes activities that enable learners to see themselves as others see them (peer appraisal, independent recording of activity, video and audio recordings, etc.). Their judgements are aided by presenting them with pen portraits of different people and deciding on a best-fit to themselves, being encouraged to express their feelings about what is right and wrong, being comfortable enough to disclose to teachers and peers, etc. Finally, learners should be encouraged through example and explanation to self-reward. All these aspects arise naturally from a classroom environment built on the principles underpinning the social and emotional aspects of learning (Weare and Gray, 2003).

An important observation: when learners are making judgements about themselves they will be using a standard. If those standards are too low then it may lead to inappropriate behaviours or insufficient activity. If those standards are too high, and the learners fail themselves repeatedly in all areas of life, then it can lead to a preponderance of negative feelings. Those negative feelings can have a poor effect upon behaviour including aggression, over-compliance or avoidance of issues.

Avoiding the limitations

Positive reinforcement is a powerful technique for changing behaviour and establishing an environment in which the learners are most prepared for learning. But sometimes the influence is reduced by the nature of its implementation. Reinforcement is not effective under four main conditions: the reinforcer losing its reinforcing nature; the reinforcement not being consistently applied; the expectations of the system; and the response of the individual to the reinforcement programme.

The reinforcer not reinforcing is a common occurrence when first establishing classroom strategies. Simply choosing the wrong reinforcer in the first instance can be the problem. Under the Premack Principle we would assume that being given permission to listen to an MP3 player in class would be reinforcing but the classroom is a complex social place and the learner may in fact not appreciate the attention or approval of the teacher. There may be over-saturation of the reinforcer; the learner is receiving too much reward and it is devalued. In the case of a token economy, one teacher may be rewarding with tokens and benefitting from the deferred personal praise by the learner's form tutor. However, if too many teachers are issuing tokens or one teacher is issuing an inflated number of tokens, then the single token ceases to be of value. (These issues are discussed further under 'Token economy'.)

The reinforcement being inconsistent can have a negative impact upon its effectiveness. The consistency or expectation of reinforcement is a crucial element. The reinforcement does not have to be instantaneous or continuous; successful programmes can be established with scheduled and deferred rewards. However, without the explicit expectation of scheduled or deferred rewards then the reinforcement should be immediate and continuous with the appropriate behaviour.

The too much, too soon situation arises when the behaviour-change expectations are too great to be achieved by the learner. This can be avoided by careful task analysis of the curriculum or behaviour and ensuring the steps of any shaping programme are small enough for the learner to accomplish. No amount of reward can enable someone to achieve the impossible, and so the reinforcement is doomed to fail. A simple example of over-expectation would be the learner having to remain focused on work for the whole lesson when recent experience has been that he interrupts lessons almost continuously. The same learner might meet a problem in a carefully prepared shaping programme if the expectation in Miss Long's class is the same as in Mr Short's class, yet the social and reinforcement conditions are very different. Again, in the early stages of developing behaviour-change and learning programmes it is easy to make the steps too large and the expectations unachievable.

Finally, the learner's attitude towards the programme can have a negative effect. Although we can design programmes, manipulate the environment and issue rewards, the overall response of a learner is also dependent upon their attitudes and motivations that are impacted upon from a number of directions. This can be considered as a cost–benefit analysis (Gillette *et al.*, 2000; Andrews, 2006), balancing the rewards against the costs. The learner may balance the benefits of the teacher recognition against, for example, their freedom of movement, freedom of choice or social status.

Reducing unwanted behaviours

Behaviourism and, in particular, behaviour modification focus upon promoting behaviours and creating effective learning situations. However, in real classrooms there is also a need to eliminate behaviours that are detrimental to learning. An individual's behaviour can affect their own learning or that of others in the rest of the class. Skinner believed that punishment could not extinguish inappropriate behaviour but there are a number of steps that can be taken to change behaviour through the use of aversives. Because punishment often has negative effects it is important that the aversives are not seen as punishments. There are four popular methods: extinction, differential reinforcement of other behaviours, reinforcement of other behaviours and punishment.

Extinction is the removal of reinforcement of behaviour to reduce the frequency or probability, or to eliminate it altogether. The process is, from theory, very simple: ignore the unwanted behaviour. In practice, if it were that simple then we would not be suffering from any unwanted behaviours! The process requires thought and management. First, it is important to identify the exact nature of the behaviour in terms of what, how, where, when and, most importantly, under what circumstances. The question 'why' can be problematic if one strays from the purely behaviourist considerations into the psychometric, socio-psychology field, but the general principle is that the behaviour, whether or not driven by a desire for attention, is positively reinforced by attention.

If appropriate, a baseline measure would be established. Although it is more usual when promoting behaviour when the information is needed to draw up a suitable contract and target for the learner, observing the behaviour, its frequency and identifiable triggers. Once the nature of the behaviour to be reduced is established then plans can be made which may not necessarily include extinction. Simply identifying the prompts and removing or reducing those has a direct impact upon the unwanted behaviour. The extinction strategy means ignoring the unwanted behaviour. An example is presented in the vignettes of the final chapter where Steven, an adult student training to be a teacher, makes unnecessary and off-focus interruptions in group discussions. Part of the strategy is to ignore the inappropriate. Responding to and allowing the discussion to be led by his interruptions would reinforce the activity. Either ignoring the focus of his interruption or totally ignoring that he has spoken is the extinction strategy in action. Obviously, the behaviourist teacher will respond with positive reinforcement if he makes a relevant comment or contribution to the discussion (appropriate behaviour). Another example is a 17-year-old student; even though he has been asked not to, he continues to write personal comments about his teachers at the side of and within his notes. In response to his teachers' further instructions or directions, he changes his behaviour so that he is obeying the exact rules but still managing to make comments or other distractions. In this case the teachers agree that his behaviour should no longer lead to reinforcement. By ignoring the inappropriate behaviour, extinction of the behaviour may occur.

Differential reinforcement is a procedure where the learner is reinforced for not exhibiting a particular behaviour. To implement this technique there has to be agreement regarding the conditions of compliance. For example, a learner is rewarded for not interrupting another pupil during the peer assessment session. That simple statement includes the behaviour and the duration of the compliance. The learner is rewarded if the condition is met.

Promoting incompatible alternative behaviour is a way of reducing an unwanted behaviour. For example, a pupil that persistently drops litter is given a responsibility in the litter picking team and receives positive reinforcement for his contribution to the management of the team.

Some behaviour modification techniques also use negative consequences for inappropriate or 'bad' behaviours. The term 'bad' evokes some moral judgement about the person or the behaviour. In behaviourist terms the word 'inappropriate' encompasses both the ethical rule-breaking and the moral sinning. The term 'negative consequences' is a euphemism for punishment, and many have been outlined in the previous chapter on theory. In those situations, behaviour modification works by conditioning learners to expect positive reactions or reinforcement to appropriate behaviour and to expect to be punished for inappropriate behaviour.

Many behaviourists believe that punishment is less of an influence upon behaviour than reward and that reward alone will be just as effective. The following is a personal note reflecting upon over 30 years of behaviourists driven teaching from infants through to adults:

I do not believe that punishment works but it is something I do and something that is necessary.

I have a belief that punishment does not work.

That belief arises from being told by my teachers when training to be a teacher, my tutors when studying in higher education and the literature. I believe it because personal experience tells me. When I've punished someone, I remember the many times that it has had no positive outcome and many times it has alienated the personal relationships.

In my first week of teaching in a secondary school, I was walking down the corridor and a senior teacher came out of his office and told me to go in to be a witness. For the first and last time I was party to corporal punishment. The boy was given three lashes with a cane – that was upsetting but the moving part was reading the punishment book that I was required to sign. That boy's name appeared many times in the book. And there were other names appearing more than once on a page. The caning certainly was not having an impact upon those being caned.

At the age of 10 years I was caned – just one formal and hard cane across the hand given because I was not standing still in line at the end of playtime. It was a snowy day and we'd been making a snowman. The snow was compacted into my woollen gloves and I was picking the lumps of snow off because I knew if I did not then the snow would melt and give me wet gloves. The resentment is still there nearly a half century later.

I punish others. I certainly shout and sometimes get upset. I show my displeasure, annoyance, frustration and anger, and I attempt to place guilt on the other person. In the main, it is not an automatic response. It is controlled and measured and apparently natural. And, lots of other teachers do it. I have no explanation as to why I punish. There are different sorts of punishment: punishment that hurts the offender like caning, smacking and emotionally upsetting them; and punishment that restricts or confines the offender, for example, sitting them away from the others, sending them to another place, keeping them back at the end of the lesson, putting them in an after-school detention, etc. There is also the punishment that is associated with the removal of the pleasant. I think there is a construct or spectrum of punishment that at one end I would not condone and, at the other, I would not find unacceptable.

A currently popular intervention is time-out. It is a form of punishment where the learner is removed from a positively rewarding environment and they are ignored and not allowed to interact with others. It is in the least unacceptable part of the spectrum of punishments.

Punishment is necessary. I have a belief, arising from experience that punishment works in one particular way. The belief is that the sight of someone being punished affects the behaviour of the others; it is the vicarious aspects of conditions and the impact of witnessing punishment. But then, why should people be forced to behave in a particular way through fear of being punished. That is certainly not in the spirit of self-efficacy.

And so, I do not believe that punishment works but it is something I do and something that is perhaps necessary.

Summary

An effective pedagogy based upon behaviourist approaches focuses upon two areas: the presentation of the curriculum and the preparedness of the learners. The curriculum is made ready for the learners by task analysis and the creation of activities that are focused and achievable. The learners are prepared for learning through positive reinforcement and, if necessary, the use of aversives. The teacher introduces teaching methods that are positively reinforcing to the learners and provide focus and reward through success, celebration and progress. The six steps to classroom success are:

1 understand the aims of the curriculum;
2 then identify clearly stated objectives (task analysis, chunking, milestones, SMART);
3 adopt mastery learning techniques (task analysis, rote, reinforcement);
4 use assessment for learning (feedback, immediacy of response);
5 positively reinforce achievement (immediacy, reward, tokens, praise);
6 encourage self-efficacy through self-rewards.

These lead to the celebration, recording and reporting of success (closure).

Activities

- Consider, in the light of the content of the chapter, the important aspects of the behaviourist pedagogy and how they could be translated into teaching strategies.
- Consider the affordances of these strategies of behaviourism: task analysis; modelling; base-lining; rote learning and contracts.

5

Strategies

By the end of this chapter you will be able to:

- make informed choices about the selection of behaviourist-based pedagogic approaches to classroom activities;

and you will have:

- reflected on the vignettes presented in the light of the preceding chapters and in the light of the commentaries.

A century is such a long time, especially in educational development and thinking; the following words, written by John Watson, echo ominously around giving behaviourism an air of narrowness, authoritarian and threatening dogmatism:

> Give me a dozen healthy infants, well-formed, and my own specified world to bring them up in and I'll guarantee to take any one at random and train him to become any type of specialist I might select – doctor, lawyer, artist, merchant-chief and, yes, even beggar-man and thief, regardless of his talents, penchants, tendencies, abilities, vocations and the race of his ancestors. (1928: 82)

Classical conditioning began this story but radical behaviourism saw the development of behaviour modification procedures that underpinned much pedagogy in the middle phases of the last century. At the height of the behaviourists' influence on pedagogy, the educational establishment became more conscious of the role of the social and the understanding of the biology of the brain; constructivist and cognitivist ideas started to dominate the pedagogy. The new millennium can see the return of pedagogy based upon behaviourism and principles tried and tested decades before. From those principles of learning, considered in detail earlier, and rooted in reported practice in the classroom, there emerges a set of strategies. We do not always knowingly design a learning activity that is based on the underlying principles; we do the planning by instinct and from a standpoint of experience of what we know works well. As teachers, we look to pragmatic ways of encouraging and ensuring learning, and in this chapter we will consider some of those strategies and give some illustrations of the principles of behaviourism in practice.

Strategies of a behaviourist teacher

This section will outline some of the approaches taken by teachers who have learned that the behaviourist approach to teaching and learning meets the needs of learners. In the behaviourist classroom some, or all, of the following approaches to encouraging learning will be evident. The teacher will:

- have clearly structured the learning intention and outcomes (task analysis);
- make use of activities that stimulate, motivate and reward the pupils (positive reinforcement);
- observe and record positive and appropriate responses in the beginning (baselining);
- make explicit the expected outcomes and behaviours (SMART targets);
- reward achievement in a systematic and fair way (token economy);
- enter into agreements to support pupils' learning (contracts);
- provide the appropriate opportunities for pupils to be in alternative places (sanctuary); and
- set a good example in terms of physical appearance and behaviour and in terms of cognitive rehearsals (modelling).

A teacher who values the principles of behaviourism and radical behaviourist theory will utilise all of the above approaches with the intention of assisting in the process of learning. They are based on the behaviourist premise that learning comes about more effectively and efficiently when it is structured, sequenced and rewarded. Bearing in mind that any individual teacher is likely to use a range of different approaches to encourage learning, the following approaches to organising learning activities in classrooms will be evident when a teacher has a bias towards directing learning in a behaviourist way. Characteristics of some lessons and parts of lessons include:

- working in silence;
- carrying out repetitive activities to develop speed and accuracy;
- learning by rote through chanting, song, rhyme or physical actions;
- kinaesthetic activities related to the theme, topic or concept;
- clearly defined outcomes;
- extrinsic rewards for completing tasks;
- recognition of success through praise and celebration; and
- charts, displays and record books emphasising successes.

Punishment will not play a significant role in the behaviourist classroom. The rules will be made clear and individuals who find it difficult to work within the accepted framework will be subject to a range of explicit formal or informal contracts relating reward to appropriate behaviour.

A small range of vignettes now illustrates these principles.

House points and the lottery draw

This vignette describes an aspect of the token economy approach to rewarding appropriate behaviour and achievement by issuing tokens. Many schools employ systems of rewards for pupils, usually in the form of stickers or merit cards. The token economy is established when the collection of the tokens leads to some higher tangible reward. For some, that is simply the increased status of the class in the school system, for others, it is the receipt of certificates or tangibles on an individual basis. The following vignette describes the token economy at an ordinary state comprehensive secondary school. The interesting feature is the way in which the tokens are exchanged for tangible rewards.

Thorndale School is an 11–16 comprehensive school in southern England with 750 pupils and six forms in each year. The academic achievement is above the local average and well above the national average. The pupils attend from a wide rural area. The token economy is based on merits that are awarded to individual pupils for a number of reasons:

- achievement in extra-curriculum sporting activity;
- performance at a single event (for example, participating in the school play);
- doing better than expected (ipsative assessment) on a test, examination, homework exercise or project; and
- behaving better than usual.

The merits are usually awarded singly but awards of 5, 10 or even 20 credits are possible for outstanding activity, for example, appearing in the local newspaper for winning a dog show prize. Occasionally merits are awarded to groups of pupils – each pupil receives the same allocation. For example, the whole class may be given a merit point for completing an activity in a particularly efficient way.

Periodically, once every term, the tokens are placed together for a grand draw or lottery. The prizes are significant; included in one draw were family tickets to local theme parks, and £10 and £20 vouchers for local stores. In total the value of the term's lottery draw prizes would be in the order of £500 although much came from school benefactors and all came through the parents' association.

Many pupils are highly motivated to collect merits – the 'you have to be in it to win it' enticement was evident when speaking to the pupils.

The school was motivated to enhance the merit system because there was a perceived lowering of engagement by the pupils in lessons. This manifested itself in low-level off-task behaviour, poorer standards of homework and poorer behaviour around the school during break times. The overall benchmark standards of the school were falling.

The individual merit system has the advantage over 'house-' or 'form-based' systems in that the reward remains with the individual. However, because a whole class, form, team or after-school club can receive a merit or several merits, there is also an encouragement to work for the team and classroom collaboration.

Some token systems are susceptible to devaluation through inflation. Devaluation is when the value of the token is diminished because of the increased numbers that are issued. From an analytical point of view, this system would be subject to inflation, as there seems to be no limit to the numbers of merits that can be issued. The lottery element of the distribution of the reward seems to hide this from the perceptions of the pupils. This form of behaviour modification was described by Skinner in his analysis of schedules of conditioning. It is a fixed-interval schedule whereby the delay in reward is significant but the period is predictable. In animal experiments he and others noticed that it causes high amounts of responding near the end of the interval (just before the lottery draw), but much slower responding immediately after the delivery of the reinforcer (Dews, 1978). (Author's note: I have not been able to identify any similar research data relating to fixed-interval scheduling in school-based token economies – this vignette describes a successful strategy but it does not have rigorous data.)

Basic skills, basic methods

The early work of behaviourists such as Thorndike and Skinner extrapolated their findings with animals to the application of the principles in education. They related the simple stimulus–response mechanisms directly to teaching practices. A characteristic of many strategies is repetition. Ebbinghaus studied the impact of different schedules of rote learning and their value to sustained memory. There are some key skills that all children need to possess if they are to become efficient and effective learners. One of those is being able to learn to spell new words. This next vignette describes one such method.

The learning support area of Ashley Middle School (pupils aged 9 to 13 years) has five classes in each year and covers teaching in Key Stage 2 and Key Stage 3 of the UK National Curriculum. Specialist teachers teach most subjects but all teachers teach their form English, mathematics and ICT. They teach humanities or science to their form according to their specialism. Specialist teachers teach PE, music, drama and design technology. There is a learning support area; pupils are extracted from lessons to be given one-to-one tuition, small group work or pastoral support. There is a large team of learning assistants giving in-class support to individuals or the class in general; their work is coordinated through the learning support area. The learning support assistants are trained in a range of strategies to support specific spelling, reading and writing difficulties, one of which is a kinaesthetic approach to the learning of spellings.

The two keywords associated with this strategy for learning to spell a new word are repetition and kinaesthetic. Importantly, the words to be learned are copied by the pupil in a clear cursive style as a single sequence of fine finger movements from start to finish. This is the model for them to follow, for example, importantly, sequence and kinaesthetically (below). The process is one of 'Look, say and trace. Cover, say and write. Check and repeat'. The learner reads aloud, emphasising the syllables and tracing the pen over the letters in turn. They then cover the word and say aloud re-emphasising the syllables. They look and check again. They cover and say aloud and write the word in cursive text, saying the syllables as the letters are written. In the first stages the learner may say and copy with the original word exposed; in the final stages they may simply look, say, cover and write. The emphasis is on the saying, that is, the extenuated and slow statement of the syllables as the word is written in cursive (joined-up) writing.

The approach was adopted because the school had identified correct spelling as an important skill for children to learn. Teaching the children to be independent spellers gives them confidence.

The approach is multisensory and suits many learning styles:

- *visual* – the shape of the individual letters and the outline of the whole words;
- *auditory* – allowing the child to break down a complex-sounding word into simple phonic units; and
- *kinaesthetic* – finger-tracing words, writing words and cursive handwriting.

The approach can be part of an integrated approach with other strategies like 'Imagine your eyes are a camera, look at the word and take a picture, imagine the word in your mind'.

This kinaesthetic approach to spelling requires a great deal of effort on the part of the learner and the motivation to succeed. The success of completing a part or whole word correctly is the positive reinforcer that the learners generate for themselves. The teacher can add to the positive reinforcement by praising the use of the correct procedure and praising the perseverance of the learner. The word is 'remembered' through the association of the sound, the movement of the finger/pen and the look of the letters formed. The scheduling and repetitive nature of the task reinforces the learning process

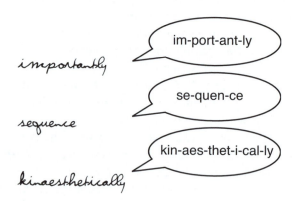

Figure 5.1 Learning to spell

with pupils returning to previously learned words to reinforce their memory and reinforce confidence in the process by further successful activity.

Books, research papers and practical advice on the teaching of spelling often argue that irregular words should be learnt by a variety of 'look, cover, write' methods. Ann Cooke (1998) has written an analysis of a number of these methods but is critical of some methods because they disregard the grammar and syntax associated with spelling and reading; the contextual clues are important for successful reading of individual words. Some methods 'do not consider the multisensory nature of language functioning' (Cooke, 1998: 240). The behaviourist approach described above is multisensory, it promotes self-efficacy and it facilitates positive reinforcement of appropriate behaviours.

Computer-based spelling programs have been promoted over the past 30 years, many of them based upon the behaviourist principles associated with the immediacy of the positive reinforcement of correct responses and valued because of their facility to give accurate feedback to the learner without the presence of the teacher. They are also seen to be more motivating as the media of learning is attractive to young people and the rewards can be games or game-like activities. In recent years, the programs have become web-based, such as the following which are available online:

- http://www.bbc.co.uk/skillswise/words/spelling/waystolearn/look cover/game.shtml
- http://www.amblesideprimary.com/ambleweb/lookcover/lookcover. html

However, these programs lack the kinaesthetic, visual and auditory support for spelling that is associated with handwritten work. Many use a font that is very different from the pupil's style of writing.

Shaping and modelling in ICT teaching

Shaping and modelling are two very different behaviourist approaches but are associated because the strategies that arise from those principles can be similar. Strategies arising from shaping make the learner carry out the behaviour, usually with repetition, through steps that enable the learning to get closer and closer to the desired outcome. Modelling as a strategy is showing the learner what to do; they learn by direct copying or subconscious imitation.

Shaping and modelling in ICT teaching is a common occurrence. Many lessons start with an introductory session where the teacher demonstrates the activities and outcomes to the pupils. In the better-taught lessons, the process does not include a complete step-by-step demonstration of every movement – many pupils will become demotivated as they experience no positive feedback from the session. They are unlikely to remember every step demonstrated. In the better-taught lessons the teacher is drawing upon prior experience and learned skills and is chaining those together in a novel way to achieve the outcome. In these good lessons, pupils learn that ICT is the application of the skills they already possess, in new situations. It is that attitude reflected in their use of computers that is called ICT capability.

After the introduction in which the desired outcome is modelled, the pupils will often work alone on the computer, seeking help when required. It is important that they receive a sustained level of positive reinforcement. The main source is from the success they achieve – that is intrinsic reinforcement – but some pupils may need the motivation of extrinsic reinforcement. The teacher's task is to provide reinforcement of those appropriate behaviours of learning and attainment in preference to positively reinforcing inappropriate behaviours.

Appropriate behaviours include making progress, solving problems, achieving outcomes, supporting others, being on-task, being attentive to the instruction given by the teacher and so on. The behaviourist teacher will have reinforcers in place that increase the probability of those behaviours reoccurring. Having a worksheet that itemises the milestones of the activity can reinforce the progress of the learner; they tick each item as it is achieved. That same sheet can also be used as a record of when and how they solved a problem and as a record of the help they gave to another pupil. The teacher's role is to positively reinforce the pupils' recording activities, either through praise, the use of systematic reward tokens, simple acknowledgement of success or the celebration of that success.

Inappropriate behaviours include being out of their seat, being off-task, talking to another about an off-task topic, interfering with another person's computer and doing inappropriate activities on the computer. These behaviours are extinguished by not being positively reinforced. Many actions of the teacher can inadvertently cause the reinforcement; for example, shouting across the classroom 'Darren, this is the fortieth time I've told you to stay in your seat' may be a positive reinforcer as Darren likes the attention and his out–of–seat behaviour will continue. Similarly, being off-task, talking about off-task topics and doing inappropriate things on the computer can be inadvertently reinforced. A means of suppressing the inappropriate is by making the appropriate much more dominating; that is called counter conditioning. Counter conditioning is when 'behavior that is incompatible with the behavior to be weakened is available and easily reinforced' (MacMillan, 1973: 79). In the case of Darren, it is by making the positive reinforcers of the appropriate behaviour more powerful, appropriate to Darren's needs – perhaps a contract or agreement whereby the teacher will always go and tick his sheet every time he reaches a milestone or makes an achievement like solving a problem.

Teaching in an ICT room has all the challenges of classroom teaching but with the added complexities of the opportunities for inappropriate behaviour caused by the technology and the demands placed upon ICT teachers to be able to diagnose the computer errors of pupils and enable them to get the learner back to a point from which they can progress.

SEAL, sanctuary and self-efficacy

Even in our normal classrooms we have pupils showing emotional and behavioural difficulties. Obviously behaviour modification techniques are appropriate strategies for the teachers to use with those pupils and the pupils in their classes. In this example, the secondary school also employed the strategy of sanctuary. The learner is given the opportunity to 'escape' in a pre-arranged contract. The negotiation of that contract is an important element of the strategy as it helps the pupil identify the trigger signs of his or her behaviour. The sanctuary could be a desk away from the other pupils, sitting under the table, going to a 'chill-out' room or reporting to another member of staff.

Swanfield School is an 11–16 comprehensive school in southern England with 700 pupils and six forms in each year. The academic achievement is well below the local average and below the national average. The school is situated in a large area of social housing, and most pupils come from the local community. The school gives support for pupils with special educational needs by in-class support, tutorial counselling and using special-needs teachers to teach the lower sets in some subjects. There is an area of the school called pupil support services where special-needs teachers and pastoral leaders are based, and there are rooms for teaching groups and providing confidentiality when giving pastoral support. It is this area that provides the sanctuary.

All contracts are agreed upon on an individual basis between the pupil and a member of the pastoral support team. The contract and the actions of the pupils are monitored by that teacher. The contract gives permission for the pupil to leave the classroom and go to the sanctuary at any time they choose. They have to inform the teacher and they are expected to do that discreetly and politely. That is a significant aspect of the strategy and one that is emphasised to the pupils. The pupil has the right to choose to go to the sanctuary. The teacher would only in exceptional circumstances of safety refuse the pupil. Again, that is an important aspect of the strategy in that it gives the pupil the sense of self-efficacy that they frequently need.

On going to the sanctuary, the pupil is expected to report to a member of staff who completes the necessary records so that pupil welfare, attendance and behaviour is securely documented. The pupils would expect to settle to some form of activity such as reading, drawing, listening to audiotapes, completing puzzles or simply meditating. If it were thought to be appropriate, the teacher would engage with the pupil and enquire to the circumstances leading up to the call for sanctuary. The pupil would not normally return to the lesson unless it could be accomplished with the consent of the classroom teacher and at a time appropriate for further learning. Normally the pupil would attend the following lesson.

In Swanfield School, this is seen to be a more effective method of dealing with and resolving behaviour issues because the learner is identifying the symptoms, the triggers and the consequences of their behaviour. The situation tends to take the heat out of any encounters, and the general level of antagonistic behaviour around the school is reduced. The pupils respond positively to the situation, and the need for sanctions by the classroom teacher has been reduced. The number of pupils requiring and receiving support for emotional and behavioural difficulties is high enough to warrant the investment in the strategy. The strategy is an important element of the school's

'Every Child Matters' strategy (DfES, 2004) and their consideration of the social and emotional aspects of learning (SEAL).

It is noted that the pupil should normally remain out of the classroom until the end of the lesson. The duration of sanctuary time is an interesting consideration. In some school practices, the amount of time can be considered to be as short as minutes, simply going outside and counting to ten. The important aspect of this situation is the pupil control at the point of making the decision to escape. Thereafter, the system takes the necessary control to preserve the professional status of the teacher, the education of the pupils and the impact that a return to the class might have on the rest of the class.

It was seen in Swanfield School that, at times, some learners find the constraints, distractions and obligations of the classroom too difficult. As a result they become off-task, poorly behaved, disruptive and even a danger to themselves or others. Adopting a sanctuary method to cope with such behaviour is a positive approach to reducing disruptive behaviour in the classroom and around the school. The learners become in better control of their environment and their own behaviours, and they and the school benefit from their increased self-efficacy.

In a nearby school, the emphasis is placed upon celebration and monitoring achievement and positive behaviour through rewards and awards. They include:

- house points awarded electronically by the teacher, and the top 50 pupils are publicised on the school website;
- the pupils with the largest number of house points receive 'fun' prizes determined by the availability of funds;
- postcards are sent home by individual teachers to reward individual pieces of good work, and phone calls are made to parents on the same basis;
- jumper badges are awarded: silver and gold for consistent good effort or behaviour in subjects;
- subjects also arrange reward trips, as often as once a term, limited to the top few pupils in each class;
- award assemblies are held where plaques and certificates are awarded for attitude to learning and for most improved in each year group;
- good attendance certificates are awarded;
- there is an awards evening for the sports personality of the year; and
- there are academic awards evenings for the celebration of individual and group achievements in learning and behaviour.

Both schools reflect a great deal of effort to positively reinforce appropriate behaviour either through social status and responsibility or by recognition and reinforcement by teachers through a merit-based system.

Teacher training, social engagement

Teacher training has three significant aspects to it. There is the massive body of knowledge associated with the curriculum, regulations, expectations, procedures and policies; that is usually disseminated in lectures, handbooks and references to the professional and academic literature. There are the craft skills and confidence building associated with classroom practice, and this takes place in real schools and real classrooms with real pupils. The third element is the dissemination of information in the small group setting where trainees are able to articulate their understanding, their uncertainties, their opinions and their beliefs. It is in this situation that the vignette describes how a trainee's behaviour needs modifying so that they more readily meet the requirements of their training and are better equipped to accommodate new ideas.

Steven is 28 years old, training to be a secondary school ICT teacher after completing a biology degree and having spent 5 years in the computer industry programming and designing systems in a commercial laboratory. He is very enthusiastic about becoming a teacher and expresses an opinion on every matter raised. The training sessions are in groups of 18 to 20 trainees, and the general approach is for the lecturer to provide the structure for the sessions, provide the content in terms of information (written, presented or spoken) and chair the discussions. The degree to which Steven contributes to the discussions is excessive, dominating and dictatorial. He is not reflective upon his own opinions and his responses to others' opinions are usually adversarial.

The lecturer applied these strategies: baselining, positive reinforcement and contracting.

Baselining establishes the degree to which the inappropriate behaviour is occurring and may be necessary to 'convince' the learner that there is a problem. It certainly is necessary to establish a baseline of activity if a contract is to be drawn up. In this case, the lecturer drew a grid representing all the people in the room on which she could covertly tally the responses and interventions of the entire group. With some groups, overt tallying is a means of drawing attention to the expectation of an appropriate number of interventions by each individual. The lecturer implemented positive reinforcement of all appropriate responses (those that had an element of reflection or accommodation of another's opinion). There was no change in Steven's behaviour. The lecturer spoke directly and confidentially to Steven. She explained that the issues were over-participation, not representing the reasons for his own opinions and not accommodating the opinions of others. She also pointed out that he should demonstrate 'positive values, attitudes and behaviour' and have a 'constructively critical approach' towards new ideas. She did not enter into a formal contract but Steven was aware of the covert recording of contributions to discussions.

The result was Steven's immediate and almost complete withdrawal from participation in the sessions, but within two sessions he was again entering into the discussions, and he acknowledged, through eye contact, the lecturer's positive reinforcement of his appropriate contributions.

Steven is now a successful secondary-school teacher.

Steven is not unusual in that he represents a large number of people entering the teaching profession who possess the confidence arising from successful employment, mature ideas and vocational aspirations for the education of young people. However, some are not sensitive enough to the needs of others and the mores of schools. Consequently, their successful acceptance in schools is hampered. A teacher in particular needs to be aware of the opinions and understanding of others, especially the pupils, if they are going to be able to respond to their needs, set fitting targets, identify suitable rewards and reinforce appropriate behaviour.

Improving the learning environment

This vignette relates how behaviourist-based policies are fostering a better environment for learning and having an impact upon pupils' behaviour, both outside and within the classroom.

Henry Foster Community School is a popular suburban secondary school drawing pupils from the full range of socio-economic backgrounds. It has a small number of disruptive pupils but also has many successful academic, sporting and vocationally focused pupils. It is in the top 20 per cent of schools when measured by academic success. However, the school was suffering from low-level disruption, petty vandalism, a deteriorating décor and dirty and litter-strewn buildings and grounds. A strategy was introduced to tackle the issues.

Two needs were identified:

1 the need to set good examples for all pupils to model; and
2 the need to significantly change the behaviour of a small number of pupils.

The good example was seen to be the actions of the teachers, the overall behaviour of pupils, the care shown for the fabric of the building and the importance shown by all staff for the care of the environment. The décor refurbishment was not made to be contingent upon a change of behaviour but was part of the behaviour change strategy. Walls were painted, flooring refurbished and ceilings repaired. The caretaking staff had a renewed service level agreement that emphasised the tidiness of the premises, cleanliness of surfaces and repair of furniture. Pupils' work was displayed to celebrate success. If a display was damaged then staff would immediately remove it and replace it with an undamaged item.

Pupils were given responsibility for carrying out monitoring tasks for litter, damage to furniture, broken fittings and corridor graffiti. Tutor groups were given geographical responsibility for ensuring that the area adjacent to their room was tidy, clean and presentable. The pupils wrote codes of conduct.

Dealing with the minority of pupils involved two strategies: identifying the offenders through vigilance by staff and other pupils, and supporting their appropriate behaviour by giving responsibility for offence-related tasks. Persistent litter droppers were responsible for monitoring and collecting litter. Graffiti writers were put on wall cleaning duties. Those that were caught damaging posters had to make new posters.

So that these responses to inappropriate behaviour did not prove to be too time-consuming for staff and so that the punishment element was reduced, the activities would take place in 'social time' occurring during registration periods and the break periods during the day. The systems were mostly managed and monitored by pupils with specific responsibilities.

This strategy for dealing with the inappropriate behaviours of littering, graffiti and damage to property was dealt with using positive reinforcement of commending and celebrating learners taking responsibility for areas of the school. Negative reinforcement (the removal of an aversive) to reward learners was also employed. Pupils who were placed in detention for wrongdoing were given the opportunity to do creative or reparatory activities and to receive praise and commendation.

Computerisation of the curriculum

This vignette is a report of classroom activity taking place in the early 1980s but it can be read as a current project because it is the conversion of a curriculum from a rich description of aims and content to a set of precise and observable objectives. In terms of current behaviourism, it is the task analysis of the subject matter and the creation of a number of behavioural objectives. In terms of the current curriculum, the National Curriculum for England and Wales, it is the conversion of the key concepts, key processes and curriculum opportunities into a set of specific activities that are measureable, achievable, relevant and timely. It is the same activity taking place in every classroom, every day whereby the teacher plans activities for learners. It is that activity which is taking place when teachers and learning technologists are placing the curriculum onto a virtual learning environment (VLE). This vignette tells how the curriculum was analysed and broken into small activities, how they were sequenced and presented on the computer and how they then met the needs of pupils who benefited from the personalised curriculum. The description uses the terms of the 1980s; the translations are in italics.

Computer-managed learning (CML) is the use of a computer [*VLE*] to direct the study of the pupil when the pupil leaves the computer. This study involves the development of a computer program [*the development of VLE content*] that manages the mathematics curriculum of a class of less-able secondary school pupils over a period of 1 year. The conclusions drawn were that the computer could be used to direct pupil activities in the classroom but that there were hardware and software limitations that had to be overcome before computers in general could be used efficiently in that situation.

There was a need to introduce 'individualized teaching' [*personalisation*] into the curriculum because, although the remedial department [*learning support area*] was highly selective, there was a wide span of ability with some very weak pupils. Pupil motivation and varying work rates seemed to be important factors affecting pupil attainment. With the new intake it was usual to return to a much earlier stage of teaching. All of our pupils have to return to a very early stage (e.g. letter sounds in reading) but obviously some pupils will need to move quickly from this point whereas others will not. Individualised learning programmes are essential.

There was a need to introduce a 'more precise' teaching method because the staff covering the classes are not necessarily teachers of the less able. They perhaps are not even volunteers. Some may only have a commitment of a single or a few lessons per week. Often there is low motivation to make extensive preparation for the lessons. A scheme of approach requiring little lesson preparation was therefore necessary.

The scheme needed to utilise a wide range of textbooks and teaching materials. Various teachers had their favourite texts which they wanted to use. There was a large number of texts but only a few copies of each – not whole-class sets. Teaching materials such as weights were limited thus preventing the whole class carrying out the same activity.

As a result of the above considerations a list of 20 objectives [*learning outcomes*] was drawn up based upon the previous curriculum, the teaching materials available, the desires/interests of the pupils, the opinions of the teachers involved and a consideration of academic works on the teaching of mathematics. It was then the intention that the pupils achieve each objective in turn [*sequencing*], working at their own rate through the scheme and not moving to the next objective until they had achieved the criterion of success on the present objective. Each objective had associated with it an overall topic, a criterion of performance, several references to texts and teaching materials and a test (probe) [*assessment of learning*]. For example:

- TOPIC: Shape
- OBJECTIVE: Spell names of common 2D shapes
- CRITERION: Seven correct spellings in 1 minute
- REFERENCE: Beta 2, pages 64, 70, 74; More Practice 1, Unit 27
- TEST: A sheet of the seven shapes

Before the computerisation [*uploading of resources, also called populating*] of the scheme could begin, a consideration of all the processes in the classroom had to be made to identify those processes suitable for computerisation and those that should not be computerised. The following list was created (see the original paper [Woollard, 1984]).

The computer [*VLE*] is a very efficient data processor and therefore the storage of the lists is an obvious use of the computer. Record-keeping is simply a development of that storage facility. However, the development of pupil profiles is not as easily programmed because of the problem of objectifying a process that is still subjectively biased. Many 'failing pupils' seem to be characterised by deficits in motivation, ability and attendance. An individualised approach to teaching helps solve the problem of continuity caused by absence. Individualised teaching accommodates the creation of smaller goals and more regular positive reinforcement. Objectives allow easier task analysis and so sub-goals for the less able are more easily created.

The teacher setting work is not as valuable an act. Indeed, setting work is not a positively reinforcing action and so making the computer do the task can be to the advantage of the teacher. The pupil carrying out tasks is the aim of education. The teacher helping the pupil is the most productive and rewarding aspect of education. A primary aim of the computer [*VLE*] should be to relieve the teacher of as many tasks as possible so that the time devoted to helping the pupil is maximised.

Conclusions [*in 1984*]:

The use of computers to manage the curriculum in a particular classroom is possible. However, there must be a development of management skills and a greater understanding of the technology by teachers if the potential of the computer is to be met. Future developments of CML systems will be more successful if they utilise the more advanced computers that are now available in schools. Finally, CML will be more efficiently used as pupils, both able and less able, become more familiar with the technology that will play a more and more important role in their future lives.

The full paper provides further details of the project (Woollard, 1984) but the following statements drawn from the paper are particularly interesting from the perspective of our current use of computers and our understanding of the curriculum:

■ 'Once the classroom system is specified then the teacher can more easily communicate his or her ideas to the programmer.' We teachers of the twenty-first century can now do it for ourselves; we do not need the intervention of a computer programmer.

- 'Some objectives were hard to computerise and so measuring attainment was not efficient.' Fortunately, at the moment, the computer cannot do everything; there are some activities that any degree of task analysis and sequencing cannot operationalise and that require our intervention, understanding and motivations as teachers.

- 'Some pupils do not like using the computer', 'Abstainers can cause problems' and 'Hardware failure occurred such as tape recorders failing to record the data correctly.' Life has not changed; simply the technology has changed – we now have synchronisation issues, bandwidth annoyances and memory stick failures. In essence, pupils have not changed; we still experience amongst the digital natives those that prefer conventional methods of learning and those that abstain from all forms of learning. The use of positive reinforcement and the development of self-efficacy may have an impact.

During the intervening 25 years, teachers' use of computers has developed and we can now easily create profiles of pupils, individual and secure logins, integration of data with school information management systems, e–communication with parents and remote updating of information. The VLE has liberated the teacher and enabled the pupil. Through the behaviourist strategies of task analysis and the sequencing of activities, we can 'computerise' the curriculum. The internet and the ability to foster virtual human interaction through multi–user virtual environments (MUVE) will raise the issues of conditioning of avatars, modelling of behaviours (Bandura, 1977) and cybergogy – the pedagogy of virtual environments (Wang, 2005; Scopes, 2009).

The challenging class

This final vignette retells the story of a novice teacher meeting a class with a large number of challenging pupils. Michelle Harding is in her second year of teaching and newly arrived at a city school with lower-than-national average examination results, a high level of unsocial and rowdy behaviour out-of-lessons and a setting system that concentrates reluctant adolescents together. The class of 15 to 16 year olds have opted for the course in business studies but did not complete sufficient coursework previously to be entered for the examination. It is acknowledged that getting the curriculum right for the learners is very important; these strategies are the ones adopted to focus upon and deal with behaviour management.

After three most unsuccessful lessons of not engaging the pupils and having a continual battle with petty disruptive behaviour and an incident of major disruptive behaviour, the teacher sought advice from a colleague. The words are those of that colleague.

'The first step is one of task analysis. It is a question of establishing what you want to happen in the classroom and then deciding upon the sequence. The next stage is to establish a baseline measurement of the target behaviours – do that from your memory of the previous lessons. The next stage is to identify the reinforcers for the learners. Then the strategy is to introduce each of the targets in turn using continuous reinforcement and then an appropriate partial reinforcement schedule'.

After discussion and teasing out the issues, the goals that they thought were appropriate – that is, doable – and would lead to a sustained learning environment were getting the attention of the class; ensuring that the pupils were prepared for learning; enabling the pupils to deal with transitions; and helping the pupils deal with feedback about their work, including grades and marks.

The baseline measurements were established by recall of the previous lessons. 'Establishing the baseline has two purposes. It enables any progress to be recognised, which will convince and encourage you that the interventions are working, and identifies which are working best and if any do not seem to make a difference. The second reason is to make the target setting for individuals, small groups or the whole class more realistic.' That is, the targets should be neither trivial and easily achieved or too challenging and unachievable.

Identifying the reinforcers is a most important activity, using the Premack Principle that any high probability behaviour will serve as a reinforcer for any low probability behaviour. The high probability behaviours that could enhance the learning progress include using the computers, chatting in social groups, completing rote activities and making drawings and sketches. 'Which of the reinforcers can you introduce into your teaching without compromising the expectations of the school, the curriculum you are required to teach and your own teacher beliefs?'

For each of the goals, a short programme of sub-goals and a schedule for the reinforcements were established. Here are the discussions relating to getting attention:

'In some scenarios the baseline would be established with a degree of numerical accuracy. What is the current situation?'

'At the start of the lesson: pupils not going to seats, deep in conversation and ignoring my pleas for quiet, my having to shout and then not getting everyone's attention'.

'Knowing the pupils, the context and curriculum as well as the principles of behaviourism is very important. Consider, what do they do? Come in the room, talk, sit, play on the computers ... All of these are positive reinforcers so you need to establish a routine that is reinforced by those activities. At the start of the lesson, have them wait outside with you just inside the room. When they are settled, allow them in slowly, control the flow by engaging in positive conversation with the person about to enter the room. Turn your attention to the room, smiling as they *stand* behind their desks. Drop your smile to a frown towards someone who is too loud or out of place. Ask for attention and immediately reward the attention by what you say. It should not be the punishment of "Stop talking"; it should be the positive reinforcement of "Please sit down". Call for attention; it should be reinforced by a smile and "Today, we are going to [do something interesting]". Never ask for the attention of the class, group or individual to give a punishment – they will learn not to give attention. Whenever you are going to ask for attention, first consider what the positive reinforcement is going to be – what nice thing you will say first.'

'Consider negative reinforcers – that is, the removal of something bad to reinforce an appropriate behaviour. If it is in your power to reduce the homework commitment, use it to reward for appropriate behaviour in the lesson. Do NOT say, "If you are good then I will not set homework", because then, if some pupils misbehave, the homework becomes a punishment for every pupil. Use it after the appropriate behaviour as a reward – instead of the ten questions set for homework at the start of the lesson you tell them that because they have worked well the homework is reduced to just five questions of their own choice from the ones set. Homework can become part of the reward system!'

'Scheduling is important, that is, the pattern of reinforcement aligned with the strategies and goals that are introduced. At the start you will need to continuously reinforce appropriate behaviours. Getting attention is a key goal but it will be using all your reinforcers. You need to reduce the reinforcement for that goal by intermittently reinforcing. You could reinforce less often or you could introduce delays between the appropriate responses and the reinforcement, for example, delaying the praise signal when getting their attention by telling them some important piece of information.'

'Michelle, this is not easy. It takes a lot of time analysing what is going on in the classroom, noting how the pupils are responding to you [becoming a reflective practitioner], establishing priorities as clearly expressed goals, devising sequences of activities to meet those goals, identifying the reinforcers and using them in a strategic way.'

Michelle learned that the principles, when put into practice, worked and she established the routines in her classroom for that particular class. She also saw that establishing the same routines for her more biddable classes also gave benefits in that they too became more quickly focused upon learning. She was also able to apply the principles of positive reinforcement to promote and instil higher-level learning techniques associated with speed, depth and scope of working. She was also able to introduce much higher levels of pace, increase the quantity of writing, create intense but controlled discussions and get learners to represent other people's points of view. She realised that behaviourism was not just for the badly behaved.

Activities

- Compare your teaching practice with one of the vignettes and consider how you could enhance teaching and learning by adopting the pedagogic principles.
- Consider how vignettes representing good teaching practice outside of the context of your teaching could be adapted and made usable by you.
- Considering your own teaching, which aspect of it most closely follows behaviourist principles? How could your teaching be represented by a vignette?

References

ABAI. (2009). Association for Behavior Analysis International. Online. Available HTTP <http://www.abainternational.org/BAinPractice.asp> (accessed November 9, 2009).

Ader, R. (2000). 'On the development of psychoneuroimmunology'. *European Journal of Pharmacology*, 405(1–3), 167–76.

Aeschleman, S. R., Rosen, C. C. and Williams, M. R. (2003). 'The effect of non-contingent negative and positive reinforcement operations on the acquisition of superstitious behaviors'. *Behavioural Processes*, 61(1–2), 37–45.

Ammerman, R. T. and Hersen, M. (2001) *Handbook of Child Behavior Therapy in the Psychiatric Setting*. New York: Wiley.

Anderson, L. W. and Krathwohl, D. R. (2001). *A Taxonomy for Learning, Teaching and Assessing: A Revision of Bloom's Taxonomy of Educational Objectives*. New York: Longman.

Andrews, P. W. (2006). 'Parent-offspring conflict and cost–benefit analysis in adolescent suicidal behavior'. *Human Nature*, 17(2), 190–211.

Ariely, D. and Wertenbroch, K. (2002). 'Procrastination, deadlines, and performance: self-control by precommitment'. *Psychological Science*, 13(3), 219–24.

Bandura, A. (1965). 'Influence of models' reinforcement contingencies on the acquisition of imitative responses'. *Journal of Personality and Social Psychology*, 1(6), 589–95.

Bandura, A. (1969). *Principles of Behavior Modification*. New York: Holt, Rinehart and Winston.

Bandura, A. (1973). *Aggression: A Social Learning Analysis*. Englewood Cliffs, NJ: Prentice Hall.

Bandura, A. (1977). *Social Learning Theory*. New York: General Learning Press.

Bandura, A. (1997). *Self-Efficacy: The Exercise of Control*. New York: Freeman.

Bandura, A. and Walters, R. H. (1959). *Adolescent Aggression*. New York: Ronald.

Bandura, A. and Walters, R. H. (1963). *Social Learning and Personality Development*. New York: Holt, Rinehart and Winston.

Bandura, A., Ross, D. and Ross, S. (1961). 'Transmission of aggression through imitation of aggressive models'. *Journal of Abnormal and Social Psychology*, 63(3), 575–82. Online. Available HTTP <http://psy.ed.asu.edu/~classics/Bandura/bobo.htm> (accessed November 9, 2009).

Baucum, D. (1996). *Psychology*. New York: Barron's Educational Series.

Baum, W. M. (2005). *Understanding Behaviorism: Behavior, Culture, and Evolution*. Oxford: Wiley-Blackwell.

Bayley, N. (1955). 'On the growth of intelligence'. *American Psychologist*, 10(12), 805–18.

Becker, W. C., Madsen, C. H., Arnold, C. R. and Thomas, D. R. (1967). 'The contingent use of teacher attention and praise in reducing classroom behavior problems'. *Journal of Special Education*, 1(3), 287–307.

Bickel, W. K. and Vuchinich, R. (2000) *Reframing Health Behavior Change with Behavioural Economics*. Mahwah, NJ: Erlbaum.

Bloom, B. S. (1956). *Taxonomy of Educational Objective, Handbook 1: Cognitive Domain*. New York: Longman.

Bloom, B. S. (1968). 'Learning for mastery'. *Evaluation Comment*, 1(2), 1–12.

Bloom, B. S. (1974). 'An introduction to mastery learning theory'. In J. H. Block (Ed.), *Schools, Society, and Mastery Learning* (pp. 3–14). New York: Holt, Rinehart and Winston.

Boeree, C. G. (2006). *Personality Theories – Albert Bandura*. Online. Available HTTP <http://www.social-psychology.de/do/pt_bandura.pdf> (accessed November 9, 2009).

Bouton, M. E. (2000) 'A learning theory perspective on lapse, relapse, and the maintenance of behavior change'. *Health Psychology*, 19, 57–63.

Bray, M. A. and Kehle, T. J. (2001) 'Long-term follow-up of self-modeling as an intervention for stuttering'. *School Psychology Review*, 30, 135–41.

Bucklin, B. R. and Dickinson, A. M. (2001) 'Individual monetary incentives: a review of different types of arrangements between performance and pay'. *Journal of Organizational Behavior Management*, 21(3), 45–137.

Burton, D. and Bartlett, S. (2006) 'Shaping pedagogy from psychological ideas'. In D. Kassem, E. Mufti and J. Robinson, *Education Studies: Issues and Critical Perspectives* (pp. 44–5). Milton Keynes, UK: Open University Press.

Cattell, P. (1960). *The Measurement of Intelligence of Infants and Young Children*. New York: Psychological Corp.

Charlop-Christy, M. H., Le, L. and Freeman, K. A. (2000). 'A comparison of video modeling with in vivo modeling for teaching children with autism'. *Journal of Autism and Developmental Disorders*, 30(6), 537–52.

Chomsky, N. (1957). *Syntactic Structures*. The Hague: Mouton.

Cooke, A. (1998). 'Learning to spell difficult words: why look, cover, write and check is not enough'. *Dyslexia*, 3(4), 240–43.

Cozby, P.C. (2007). *Methods in Behavioral Research*. New York: McGraw-Hill Higher Education.

Dancy, J. (2000). *Practical Reality*. New York: Oxford University Press.

Darch, C. and Gersten, R. (1985). 'The effects of teacher presentation rate and praise on LD students' oral reading performance'. *British Journal of Educational Psychology*, 55(3), 295–303.

Davis, F. D. and Yi, M. Y. (2004) 'Improving computer skill training: behavior modeling, symbolic mental rehearsal, and the role of knowledge structures'. *Journal of Applied Psychology*, 89(3), 509–23.

DES (1983). *Curriculum 11–16: Towards a Statement of Entitlement: Curriculum Reappraisal in Action*. London: HMSO.

Dews, P. B. (1978). 'Studies on responding under fixed-interval schedules of reinforcement: II. the scalloped pattern of the cumulative record'. *Journal of Experimental Analysis of Behavior*, 29(1), 67–75.

DfES (2002). *Training Materials for the Foundation Subjects*. London: Department for Education and Skills.

DfES (2004). *Every Child Matters: Change for Children*. London: Department for Education and Skills.

Doane, K. R. (1959). 'Differences between pupils with good sitting posture and pupils with poor sitting posture'. *Journal of Educational Research*, 52(8), 313–17.

Du Nann Winter, D. and Koger, S. (2004). *The Psychology of Environmental Problems*. New York: Psychology Press.

Dunn, L. M. (1981). *Peabody Picture Vocabulary Test*. Circle Pines, MI: American Guidance Service.

Ebbinghaus, H. (1885). *Memory: A Contribution to Experimental Psychology*. New York: Dover Publications. Online. Available HTTP <http://psy.ed.asu.edu/~classics/Ebbinghaus/memorypref.htm> (accessed November 9, 2009).

Ewen, R. B. (1993). *An Introduction to Theories of Personality*. Hove, Sussex: Lawrence Erlbaum.

Ekman, P. (2003) *Emotions Revealed*. New York: Times Books.

Freeman, B. J., Ritvo, E. R., Needleman, R. and Yokota, A. (1985). 'The stability of cognitive and linguistic parameters in autism: a five-year prospective study'. *Journal of the American Academy of Child Psychiatry*, 24(4), 459–64.

Gardner, G. T. and Stern, P. C. (2002). *Environmental Problems and Human Behavior*. Boston: Pearson Custom Publishing.

Gesell, A. (1949). *Gesell Development Schedules*. New York: Psychological Corp.

Gillette, R., Huang, R.-C., Hatcher, N. G. and Moroz, L. L. (2000). 'Cost–benefit analysis potential in feeding behavior of a predatory snail by integration of hunger, taste and pain'. *Proceedings of the National Academy of Sciences of the United States of America PNAS*, 97(7), 3585–90.

Gottfried, J. A., O'Doherty, J. and Dolan, R. J. (2002) 'Appetitive and aversive olfactory learning in humans studied using event-related functional magnetic resonance imaging'. *Journal of Neuroscience*, 22, 10829–10837.

Graham, G. (2007). Behaviorism. In E. N. Zalta (Ed.), *The Stanford Encyclopedia of Philosophy*. Online. Available HTTP <http://plato.stanford.edu/entries/behaviorism/> (accessed November 9, 2009).

Graham, G. and Valentine, E. R. (2004). *Identifying the Mind: Selected Papers of U. T. Place*. New York: Oxford University Press.

Gureasko-Moore, S., DuPaul, G. J. and White, G. P. (2006). 'The effects of self-management in general education classrooms on the organizational skills of adolescents with ADHD'. *Behavior Modification*, 30(2), 159–83.

Hewett, F. M. (1968). *The Emotionally Disturbed Child in the Classroom: A Developmental Strategy for Educating Children with Maladaptive Behavior*. Boston: Allyn and Bacon.

Hobbes, T. (1651/2008). *Leviathan*. Oxford: Oxford University Press.

Hook, P. and Vass, A. (2004). *The Behaviour Management Pocketbook*. Alton, UK: Teachers' Pocketbooks.

Hume, D. (1748/1961). 'An enquiry concerning human understanding'. In *The Empiricists*. New York: Doubleday.

Jackson, P. (1968). *Life in Classrooms*. New York: Holt, Rinehart and Winston.

Jacobs, E. A. and Hackenberg, T. D. (2000) 'Human performance on negative slope schedules of points exchangeable for money: a failure of molar maximization'. *Journal of the Experimental Analysis of Behavior*, 73(3), 241–60.

Jena, S. P. K. (2008). *Behaviour Therapy Techniques: Research and Applications*. New Delhi: Sage.

Johnson, D. L. and Brinker, G. D. (2001) 'A comparative study of multi-component weight treatments: a replication and exploratory look at female smokers, non-smokers, and participant BMIs'. *North American Journal of Psychology*, 3, 13–30.

Johnson, M. W. and Bickel, W. K. (2003) 'The behavioural economics of cigarette smoking: the concurrent presence of a substitute and an independent reinforcer'. *Behavioural Pharmacology*, 14, 137–44.

Keinan, G. (2002) 'The effects of stress and desire for control on superstitious behavior'. *Personality and Social Psychology Bulletin*, 28(1), 102–8.

Kulik, C. L., Kulik, J. A. and Bangert-Drowns, R. L. (1990) 'Effectiveness of mastery learning programs: a meta-analysis'. *Review of Educational Research*, 60, 265–99.

Laird, J. (1968). *Hobbes*. New York: Russell and Russell.

Landsberger, H. (1958). *Hawthorne Revisited: Management and the Worker: Its Critics and Developments in Human Relations in Industry*. New York: Cornell University Press.

Lovaas, O. I. (1987). 'Behavioral treatment and normal educational and intellectual functioning in young autistic children'. Online. Available HTTP <http://rsaffran.tripod.com/lovaas1987.html> (accessed November 9, 2009).

Lovaas, O. I., Koegel, R. L., Simmons, J. Q. and Long, J. (1973). 'Some generalization and follow-up measures on autistic children in behavior therapy'. *Journal of Applied Behavior Analysis*, 6(1), 131–66.

Lovaas, O. I., Ackerman, A. B., Alexander, D., Firestone, P., Perkins, J. and Young, D. (1980). *Teaching Developmentally Disabled Children: The ME Book*. Austin, TX: Pro-Ed.

Luczynski, K. C. and Hanley, G. P. (2009). 'Do children prefer contingencies? An evaluation of the efficacy of and preference for contingent versus noncontingent social reinforcement during play'. *Journal of Applied Behavior Analysis*, 42(3), 511–25.

MacMillan, D. L. (1973). *Behavior Modification in Education*. New York: Macmillan.

Markle, S. (1969). *Good Frames and Bad: A Grammar of Frame Writing* (2nd ed.). New York: John Wiley & Sons.

Martin, G. L. and Pear, J. (2006). *Behavior Modification: What It Is and How to Do It*. Upper Saddle River, NJ: Prentice Hall.

Mattar, A. A. G. and Gribble, P. (2005). 'Motor learning by observing'. *Neuron*, 46(1), 153–60. Online. Available HTTP <http://www.cell.com/neuron/abstract/S0896-6273(05)00125-X> (accessed November 9, 2009).

Mayes, T. and de Freitas, S. (2007). 'Learning and e-learning: the role of theory'. In H. Beetham and R. Sharpe (Eds), *Rethinking Pedagogy in the Digital Age: Designing and Delivering E-learning* (pp. 13–25). London: Routledge.

Mazur, J. E. (2006). *Learning and Behavior* (6th ed.). Upper Saddle River, NJ: Prentice Hall.

McGuffin, P. W. (2006). 'The effect of timeout duration on frequency of aggression in hospitalized children with conduct disorders'. *Behavioral Interventions*, 6(4), 279–88.

Miltenberger, R. G. (2008). *Behavior Modification: Principles and Procedures* (4th ed.). Belmont, CA: Wadsworth.

Noda, W. and Tanaka-Matsumi, J. (2009). 'Effect of a classroom-based behavioral intervention package on the improvement of children's sitting posture in Japan'. *Behavior Modification*, 33(2), 263–73.

Obama, B. (2009). *Barack Obama at 100 Day Press Conference: Waterboarding is Torture*. Online. Available HTTP <http://www.youtube.com/watch?v=iMhKheewpKA> (accessed November 9, 2009).

Pajares, F. (2004). *Albert Bandura: Biographical Sketch*. Online. Available HTTP <http://des.emory.edu/mfp/bandurabio.html> (accessed November 9, 2009).

Paterson, C. R. and Arco, L. (2007). 'Using video modeling for generalizing toy play in children with autism'. *Behavior Modification*, 31(5), 660–81.

Pavlov, I. P. (1927). *Conditioned Reflexes*. London: Oxford University Press.

Pearson. (2009). *SuccessMaker*. Online. Available HTTP <http://www.pearsonschool.com/index.cfm?locator=PSZdXp> (accessed November 9, 2009).

Place, U.T. (2004). In G. Graham and E. R.Valentine (Eds), *Identifying the Mind: Selected Papers of U. T. Place*. New York: Oxford University Press.

Premack, D. (1959). 'Toward empirical behavior laws: I. Positive reinforcement'. *Psychological Review*, 66(4), 219–33.

Premack, D. (1971). 'Catching up with common sense, or two sides of a generalization: reinforcement and punishment'. In R. Glaser (Ed.), *The Nature of Reinforcement*. New York: Academic Press.

Pritchard, A. (2005). *Ways of Learning: Learning Theories and Learning Styles in the Classroom*. London: David Fulton.

Pritchard, A. (2008). *Ways of Learning: Learning Theories and Learning Styles in the Classroom* (2nd ed.). London: David Fulton.

Rayner, C., Denholm, C. and Sigafoos, J. (2009). 'Video-based intervention for individuals with autism: key questions that remain unanswered'. *Research in Autism Spectrum Disorders*, 3(2), 291–303.

Robins, L. N. (1986). 'Changes in conduct disorder over time'. In D. C. Farran and J. D. McKinney (Eds), *Risk in Intellectual and Psychosocial Development*. New York: Academic Press.

Rogers, B. (2004). *How to Manage Children's Challenging Behaviour*. London: Paul Chapman.

Rosnow, R. L. and Rosenthal, R. L. (2005) *Beginning Behavioral Research: A Conceptual Primer* (5th ed.). New York: Prentice Hall.

Rutter, M. (1970). 'Autistic children: infancy to adulthood'. *Seminar in Psychiatry*, 2(5), 435–50.

Sage. (2009). *Behavior Modification*. Thousand Oaks, CA: Sage Publications. Online. Available HTTP <http://www.sagepub.com/journalsProdDesc.nav?prodId=Journal200900>

Schultz, D. P. and Schultz, S. E. (2007). *A History of Modern Psychology* (9th ed.). Belmont, CA: Wadsworth/Thompson Learning.

Scopes, L. J. M. (2009). *Learning Archetypes as Tools of Cybergogy for a 3D Educational Landscape: A Structure for eTeaching in Second Life*. Southampton, UK: University of Southampton. Online. Available HTTP <http://eprints.soton.ac.uk/66169> (November 9, 2009).

Skinner, B. F. (1948). *Walden Two*. New York: Macmillan.

Skinner, B. F. (1950). 'Are theories of learning necessary?' *Psychological Review*, 57(4), 193–216. Online. Available HTTP <http://psychclassics.yorku.ca/Skinner/Theories> (accessed November 9, 2009).

Skinner, B. F. (1953). *Science and Human Behavior*. New York: Macmillan.

Skinner, B. F. (1968). *The Technology of Teaching*. New York: Appleton-Century-Crofts.

Skinner, B. F. (1969). *Contingencies of Reinforcement*. New York: Appleton-Century-Crofts.

Skinner, B. F. (1970). On 'having' a poem. Online. Available HTTP <http://folk.uio.no/roffe/files/Having_a_Poem.mp3> (accessed November 9, 2009).

Skinner, B. F. (1973). *Beyond Freedom and Dignity*. Harmondsworth, UK: Penguin.

Skinner, B. F. (1979). *The Shaping of a Behaviorist: Part Two of an Autobiography*. New York: Random House.

Snow, C. E. (1977). 'The development of conversation between mothers and babies'. *Journal of Child Language*, 4(1), 1–22.

Staats, A. W. (1963). *Complex Human Behavior*. New York: Holt, Rinehart and Winston.

Staddon, J. E. R. (2001). *The New Behaviorism: Mind, Mechanism, and Society*. Philadelphia, PA: Psychology Press.

Stout, R. (2006). *The Inner Life of a Rational Agent: In Defence of Philosophical Behaviourism*. Edinburgh: Edinburgh University Press.

Stutsman, R. (1948). *Guide for Administering the Merrill-Palmer Scale of Mental Tests*. New York: Harcourt and World.

TBA (2009) *The Behavior Analyst*. Online. Available HTTP <http://www.abainternational.org/TBA.asp> (accessed November 9, 2009).

Thomas, J. D., Presland, I. E., Grant, M. D. and Glynn T. L. (1978). 'Natural rates of teacher approval and disapproval in grade-7 classrooms'. *Journal of Applied Behavioural Analysis*, 11(1), 91–4.

Thorndike, E. L. (1898). 'Animal intelligence: an experimental study of the associative processes in animals'. *Psychological Review Monograph 8, Supplement 2*, 551–53.

Thorndike, E. L. and Woodworth, R. S. (1901). 'The influence of improvement in one mental function upon the efficiency of other functions'. *Psychological Review*, 8, 247–61. Online.

Available HTTP <http://psy.ed.asu.edu/~classics/Thorndike/Transfer/transfer1.htm> (accessed November 9, 2009).

Thorndike, R. L. (1972). *Manual for Stanford-Binet Intelligence Scale*. Boston: Houghton Mifflin.

Tolman, E. C. (1922). 'A new formula for behaviourism'. *Psychological Review*, 29, 44–53.

Training Development Agency (TDA) (2007) *Professional Standards for Teachers Qualified Teacher Status*. London: TDA.

TAVB (2009) *The Analysis of Verbal Behavior*. Online. Available HTTP <http://www.abainternational.org/TAVB.asp> (accessed November 9, 2009).

Vargas, J. S. (2009). *Behavior Analysis for Effective Teaching*. New York: Routledge.

Wallach, H. S., Safir, M. P. and Bar-Zvi, M. (2009). 'Virtual reality cognitive behavior therapy for public speaking anxiety: a randomized clinical trial'. *Behavior Modification*, 33(3), 314–38.

Walters, G. C. and Grusec, J. F. (1978). *Punishment*. San Francisco: W. H. Freeman.

Wang, M. (2005). 'Cybergogy for engaged learning: creating online engagement through information and communication'. The Twelfth International Conference on Learning, University of Granada, July 2005. Online. Available HTTP <http://l05.cgpublisher.com/proposals/120> (accessed November 9, 2009).

Watson, J. B. (1913). 'Psychology as the behaviorist views it'. *Psychological Review*, 20, 158–77. Online. Available HTTP <http://psychclassics.yorku.ca/Watson/views.htm> (accessed November 9, 2009).

Watson, J. B. (1928). *Behaviorism*. London: Kegan Paul, Trench, Trubner.

Weare, K. and Gray, G. (2003). *What Works in Developing Children's Emotional and Social Competence and Wellbeing?* [Research report No 456]. London: DfES. Online. Available HTTP <http://www.dcsf.gov.uk/research/data/uploadfiles/RR456.pdf> (accessed November 9, 2009).

Wechsler, D. (1974). *Manual for the Wechsler Intelligence Scale for Children, Revised*. New York: Psychological Corp.

Wenrich, W. W. (1970). *A Primer of Behavior Modification*. Belmont, CA: Wadsworth.

White, M. A. (1975). 'Natural rates of teacher approval and disapproval in the classroom'. *Journal of Applied Behavior Analysis*, 8(4), 367–72.

Whitman, T. L., Scibak, J. W., Butler, K. M., Richter, R. and Johnson, M. R. (1982). 'Improving classroom behavior in mentally retarded children through correspondence training'. *Journal of Applied Behavior Analysis*, 15(4), 545–64.

Witt, J. C. and Martens, B. K. (1983). 'Assessing the acceptability of behavioral interventions used in classrooms'. *Psychology in the Schools*, 20(4), 510–17.

Woollard, J. (1984). 'Using microcomputers with pupils with special needs: computer managed learning'. *Educational and Child Psychology*, 1(2), 124–28.

Wyatt, W. J. and Hawkins, R. P. (1987). 'Rates of teachers' verbal approval and disapproval: relationship to grade level, classroom activity, student behavior, and teacher characteristics'. *Behavior Modification*, 11(1), 27–51.

Zetou, E., Tzetzis, G., Vernadakis, N. and Kioumourtzoglou, E. (2002) 'Modeling in learning two volleyball skills'. *Perceptual and Motor Skills*, 94, 1131–1142.

Zimmerman, B. J. and Schunk, D. H. (Eds). 2002. *Educational Psychology: A Century of Contributions*. Mahwah, NJ: Erlbaum. Online. Available HTTP <http://www.des.emory.edu/mfp/ZimSchunkChpt5.pdf> (accessed November 9, 2009).

Index